WILLIAM GOLDING

A critical study

William Golding

A critical study by James R. Baker

St. Martin's Press ‡ New York

For Françoise and Christopher

Acknowledgments

Without the good will and patience of William Golding it would have been impossible to offer many of the vital facts presented in this exploratory study of his work. Mr. Golding also made it possible for me to obtain some assistance from his brother, J. T. C. Golding, and the advice of those best acquainted with his literary career: Professor Frank Kermode, Wayland Young (Lord Kennet), Charles Monteith of Faber and Faber Ltd., George MacBeth of the British Broadcasting Company, and Professor Louis D. Rubin, Jr., of Hollins College, Virginia. All interpretations, however, are my own. I am further indebted to William Golding for granting use of the essays and poems on which he holds copyright; and to William Golding and James Keating for permission to quote from the interview held at Purdue University in 1962.

I wish to thank the *Arizona Quarterly* and G. P. Putnam's Sons for allowing me to reprint the essay (only slightly revised) which now forms the first chapter of this book. Specific acknowledgment is made in the notes and in the bibliography. I am grateful to my colleagues Bruce

Woodford, Lorin Roberts, and Marvin Singleton for their sustained interest; to the San Diego State College Foundation for a useful grant-in-aid; and to all of the critics and scholars who have written on Golding's art.

For permission to quote from *Lord of the Flies* I am indebted to Faber and Faber Ltd. and to Coward-McCann, Inc. For permission to quote from *The Inheritors, Pincher Martin* (first published in the United States as *The Two Deaths of Christopher Martin*), *Free Fall,* and *The Spire* I am indebted to Faber and Faber Ltd. and to Harcourt, Brace & World, Inc. I wish to thank Faber and Faber Ltd. for permission to quote from the English edition of *The Brass Butterfly*. With this single exception, all quotations in the text of this book are taken from the first American editions.

JAMES R. BAKER

San Diego, California
December, 1964

The mind is its own place, and in itself
Can make a Heaven of Hell, a Hell of Heaven.

Paradise Lost, I, 254–55.

Contents

Preface

It would be difficult to overestimate the impact of World War II on the life and art of William Golding. He entered the Royal Navy at the age of twenty-nine in December, 1940, and after a period of service on mine sweepers, destroyers, and cruisers, he became a lieutenant in command of his own rocket ship. He saw action against the *Bismarck,* in the Atlantic convoys, in the D-day landings in Normandy, and the attack on Walcheren. As he witnessed these scenes of violence, he began to question his youthful beliefs. By the time the war ended he could no longer accept the confident scientific humanism which had been a heritage from his father and also the spirit of his training at Oxford, where he had been a student of science and literature from 1930 until 1934. But Golding did not become a war novelist. He does not write about soldiers and sailors or the great battles of the war, yet war forms the background in three of his novels—*Lord of the Flies, Pincher Martin,* and *Free Fall*—and one cannot properly assess anything he has written without taking into account that he has seen a great deal of the irrationality of men in conflict.

After the war Golding returned to his teaching position at Bishop Wordsworth's School in Salisbury, and there he worked for nearly ten years before he earned the literary reputation he possesses today. There was little enough in his early career to suggest that he would become a successful novelist. In 1930, during his Oxford days, he had published a small volume of poems in a series [1] which included the work of W. H. Auden and others who were to achieve recognition long before Golding's first novel appeared. So far as he is concerned, these youthful poems are best forgotten. Actually, they foreshadow the considerable poetic talent evident in the fiction, but they are not representative of either his mature thought or technique because they came long before the trying experiences of the war years. A few of them, nevertheless, question the neat rationalism of the scientists and historians he was reading at the time, and one suspects that the war served as a lurid confirmation of these earlier and seemingly occasional doubts. In one of these verses the poet Alexander Pope, a spokesman for the Age of Reason, projects his keen sense of order onto the universe and complains to God that not everything is perfectly arrayed. His conceit is much like that of the rational men of Golding's fables, men who will not tolerate the apparent chaos of nature and of human experience:

> Mr. Pope walked in the park—
> Trim rows of flowers
> Embroider'd the well-ordered dark
> Where marched the marshalled hours.
>
> The trees stood silent, two by two
> Pagodas lifted up their heads
> From neatly weeded laurel-groves
> And well-spaced flower beds.

1. *Poems* (London, 1934), in Macmillan's Contemporary Poets series.

> Then down a quiet gravel path—
> For Mr. Pope eschewed the sod—
> The gentleman pursued his way
> To raise his hat to Mr. God.
>
> "Dear Sir," he said, "I must confess
> This is a chastely ordered land,
> But one thing mars its loveliness,
> The stars are rather out of hand—
>
> "If they would dance a minuet
> Instead of roaming wild and free
> Or stand in rows all trim and neat
> How exquisite the sky would be!"

It was to be some time before Golding mastered the techniques of fiction which would allow him to expose, on behalf of the larger cosmos, the fatuity of the rationalist's limited vision. For ten years he made sacrifices and endured countless frustrations in the attempt to write successfully. The several novels he completed were rejected, and apparently they have disappeared forever. With the beginning of work on *Lord of the Flies,* however, he experienced a new and unaccountable confidence, but the finished manuscript seemed destined to fare little better than the early failures. It was rejected by twenty-one publishers [2] before Faber and Faber brought it out in 1954. Unpromising as it seemed, the book was immediately acclaimed in England. E. M. Forster chose it as the novel of the year, and Golding's reputation began the spectacular rise which, by 1962, carried him to fame in America as well as in England.

The Inheritors and *Pincher Martin* followed the first book within two years. Both were initially well received,

2. According to Professor Louis D. Rubin, Jr. in an unpublished commentary sent to me in October, 1962. Professor Rubin arranged for Golding's year as writer-in-residence at Hollins College, Virginia.

but enthusiasm for them waned very rapidly. The new books presented unusual difficulties for the reader: they were complex, different in form and style from the fiction of most contemporary novelists, and burdened with a philosophical significance quite alien to the modern temper. It was soon apparent to the serious critics that even *Lord of the Flies* would have to be re-examined in the light of these problems. As Golding's novels came into attention in the United States, a similar pattern of response emerged, and he earned a reputation as a difficult and sometimes obscure writer.

Only a few of his critics offered reliable interpretation. Valuable work was done in England by the scholar Frank Kermode; in the United States, John Peter's essay, "The Fables of William Golding," [3] established a pattern (and a jargon) for subsequent analysis of Golding's techniques and structures. But these critics could not stem the tide of confusion. Nor could Golding himself—though he spoke willingly of his intentions, pointed out several times that he had concentrated on Greek literature and history since the war, and that he owed very little to the main stream of contemporary literature. He wished to communicate a somewhat unorthodox picture of human nature; but, partly because he employed a traditional form in his first three books, he contributed to the impression that he was also a deeply traditional thinker. Thus many critics put him down as an old-fashioned Christian moralist. Others, confused but anxious to categorize, announced that he was an existentialist. As a result, Golding has been placed in a particularly frustrating position: *Lord of the Flies* has been hailed as a "modern classic" and it has enjoyed a phenomenal popularity through almost the entire range of the reading public; all of his work has aroused the interest of

3. *Kenyon Review*, XIX (Autumn, 1957), pp. 577–92.

intelligent scholars and critics. Yet he remains generally misunderstood.

Part of the difficulty must be traced to the popular image of Golding fabricated by the reviewers. We are shown a stern, bearded moralist who wishes to lecture to us on the sinful state of man. A product of wartime disillusionment— so the argument runs—Golding has retreated from the real problems of the modern world to take up the quaint art of allegory. And the allegories express his Calvinistic ideas through an elaborate system of parallels with Biblical lore. This newspaper fable has already proven itself inadequate to the task of interpretation, and it is difficult to believe that it can survive much longer.

The one literary influence Golding has tirelessly stressed —the influence of the Greeks—remains generally ignored. Among the many statements he has offered to publishers and interviewers over the past ten years, there is one, made during his tour of the United States, which is explicit enough to inspire the imagination of any critic: "If I really had to adopt literary parentage—I don't see why I should —but if I really had to adopt it, I should name thunderous great names like Euripides, and Sophocles, and perhaps even Herodotus. And I might go so far as to say that I have a profound admiration, illogical as it may sound, for Homer. But then, this is giving me an aristocracy of birth and upbringing I don't feel is quite justified." [4] Since Aeschylus is mentioned elsewhere, his name must be added to the list. Whether there is some specific debt to each of these writers is a matter to be examined by the classical scholars, but there is no question that the Greeks, taken collectively, represent one of the most potent forces in shaping (or confirming) Golding's conception of human psychology and human fate.

4. In an interview conducted by James Keating at Purdue University in May, 1962.

While the Greek influence is important, it does not follow that Golding is removed from the British tradition of fiction or entirely alien to the moderns. The relationships may be, as he claims, more or less fortuitous. Asked about the similarities between his *Lord of the Flies* and *High Wind in Jamaica,* he pointed out immediately that he did not encounter Hughes's island story until his own novel was finished. But the likeness did not seem to surprise him: "There is a parallel, I think, but like so many literary parallels it's a plain fact that people engaged in writing about humanity . . . are likely . . . to see something of the same thing. They're both looking, after all, at the same object, so it would really be surprising if there weren't literary parallels to be drawn between this book and that." [5]

If there is no direct borrowing, no conscious line of influence, Golding's insistence upon the limitations of rational man brings him into an English tradition which is as old as Sterne. In the Age of Reason, while Mr. Pope walked in his trim garden and deplored the unruly stars, Sterne mocked from outside.[6] It was to be more than a hundred years before that minority voice gained force and penetrated the composure of Anglo-Saxon sensibility. The protest was taken up again by the post-Victorian novelists. Among the moderns, Lawrence and Forster are prominent critics of the national consciousness; and both, finally, were to trace the imbalance and morbidity of Western man at large to the excesses of Puritanism and Rationalism in his heritage. It is hardly surprising, therefore, that Forster was the first to acclaim *Lord of the Flies;* nor is it surprising that his introduction to the American edition [7] so keenly ap-

5. In the interview by James Keating.
6. Mrs. Golding is an admirer of Jane Austen and something of an expert on the eighteenth-century novel—a worthy foil for Golding.
7. *Lord of the Flies* (New York, 1962), pp. ix–xiii.

praises the representative figures of Simon, Piggy, and Jack. As for Golding, he is not so far removed from his contemporaries as either he or his critics suggest. If there has been no deliberate borrowing on his part, he has looked at human nature and he has seen "something of the same thing"; and, if he has been influenced by the Greek tragedians more than the moderns, his vision is not entirely alien or unfamiliar to today's readers.

The pattern for this book on Golding's work emerged out of a remark he made on one occasion when he spoke with special lucidity of his intentions as a writer. The function of the artist, he said, is simply to get people "to understand their own humanity":

> He should be free enough of society to be able to see it. His place is either understanding what men are or, if he can't, trying to put before other men a recognisable picture of the mystery.
>
> The second thing a writer must have is an intransigence in the face of accepted belief—political, religious, moral— any accepted belief. If he takes one of these for granted, then he ceases to have any use in society at all. He should always be able to say, "Well, that's all very well for you but this is the picture as I see it." [8]

The second principle is certainly good advice for the critic, as well as the writer of contemporary literature. This book, therefore, takes exception to much of the published criticism on Golding, but it is not simply a rebuttal to those who have helped to shape it. The real object is to look at the whole picture in a new light.

8. In an unpublished interview conducted by Owen Webster in 1958 and sent to me through the courtesy of Mr. Charles Monteith of Faber and Faber.

WILLIAM GOLDING

A critical study

1 ‡ *Why it's no go*[1]

Lord of the Flies offers a variation upon the ever-popular tale of island adventure, and it holds all of the excitements common to that long tradition. Golding's castaways are faced with the usual struggle for survival, the terrors of isolation, and a desperate but finally successful effort to signal a passing ship which will return them to the civilized world they have lost. This time, however, the story is told against the background of atomic war. A plane carrying some English boys away from the center of conflict is shot down by the enemy and the youths are left without adult company on an unpopulated Pacific island. The environment in which they find themselves actually presents no serious challenge: the island is a paradise of flowers and fruit, fresh water flows from the mountain, and the climate is gentle. In spite of these unusual natural advantages, the children fail miser-

1. An earlier version of this chapter appears in *Arizona Quarterly,* XIX (Winter, 1963), pp. 293–305; it also appears as the "Introduction" for the *Casebook Edition of "Lord of the Flies,"* edited by James R. Baker and Arthur P. Ziegler, Jr. (New York, 1963), pp. xii–xxiv.

ably, and the adventure ends in a reversal of their (and the reader's) expectations. Within a short time the rule of reason is overthrown and the survivors regress to savagery.

During the first days on the island there is little forewarning of this eventual collapse of order. The boys (aged six to twelve) are delighted with the prospect of some real fun before the adults come to fetch them. With innocent enthusiasm they recall the storybook romances they have read and now expect to experience in reality. Among these is *The Coral Island,* Robert Michael Ballantyne's heavily moralistic idyl of castaway boys, written in 1857, yet still, in our atomic age, a popular adolescent classic in England. In Ballantyne's story everything comes off in exemplary style. For Ralph, Jack, and Peterkin (his charming young imperialists) mastery of the natural environment is an elementary exercise in Anglo-Saxon ingenuity. The fierce pirates who invade the island are defeated by sheer moral force, and the tribe of cannibalistic savages is easily converted and reformed by the example of Christian conduct afforded them. *The Coral Island* is again mentioned by the naval officer who comes to rescue Golding's boys from the nightmare island they have created, and so the adventure of these modern *enfants terribles* is ironically juxtaposed with the spectacular success of the Victorian darlings.[2]

The effect is to hold before us two radically different pictures of human nature and society. Ballantyne, no less than Golding, is a fabulist [3] who asks us to believe that the evolu-

---

2. A longer discussion of Golding's use of Ballantyne appears in Carl Niemeyer's "The Coral Island Revisited," *College English,* XXII (January, 1961), pp. 241–45.

3. See John Peter, "The Fables of William Golding." Peter distinguishes fiction from fable and classifies *Lord of the Flies, The Inheritors,* and *Pincher Martin* as "fables." Golding suggested that the term "myth" might be even better (it wouldn't), but he liked the essay and most critics are heavily indebted to it. A less simplistic view of Golding's structures is offered by Ian Gregor and

tion of affairs on his coral island models or reflects the adult world—a world in which men are unfailingly reasonable, cooperative, loving and lovable. We are hardly prepared to accept such optimistic exaggerations, but Ballantyne's tale suggests essentially the same flattering image of civilized man found in so many familiar island fables. In choosing to parody and invert this romantic image, Golding posits a reality the literary tradition has generally denied.

The character of this reality is to be seen in the final episode of *Lord of the Flies*. When the British cruiser appears offshore, the boy Ralph is the one remaining advocate of reason; but he has no more status than the wild pigs of the forest and is being hunted down for the kill. Shocked by their filth, their disorder, and the revelation that there have been real casualties, the officer, with appropriate fatherly indignation, expresses his disappointment in this "pack of British boys." There is no real basis for his surprise, for life on the island has only imitated the larger tragedy in which the adults of the outside world attempted to govern themselves reasonably but ended in the same game of hunt and kill. Thus, according to Golding, the aim of his narrative is "to trace the defects of society back to the defects of human nature"; the moral illustrated is that "the shape of society must depend on the ethical nature of the individual and not on any political system however apparently logical or respectable." [4] And, since the lost children are the inheritors of the same defects of nature which doomed their fathers, the tragedy on the island is bound to repeat the actual pattern of human history.

Mark Kinkead-Weekes in their introductory remarks for Faber's "School Edition" of *Lord of the Flies* (London, 1962). *Lord of the Flies,* they argue, evidences as many of the characteristics of fiction as it does of fable.

4. Quoted by E. L. Epstein, "Notes on *Lord of the Flies*," in *Lord of the Flies* (New York, 1959), p. 250.

The central fact in that pattern is one which we, like the fatuous naval officer, are virtually incapable of perceiving: first, because it is one that constitutes an affront to our ego; second, because it controverts the carefully and elaborately rationalized record of history which sustains the pride of "rational" man. The reality is that regardless of the intelligence we possess—an intelligence which drives us in a tireless effort to impose an order upon our affairs—we are defeated with monotonous regularity by our own irrationality. "History," said Joyce's Dedalus, "is a nightmare from which I am trying to awake." [5] But we do not awake. Though we constantly make a heroic attempt to rise to a level ethically superior to nature, and to our own nature, again and again we suffer a fall, brought low by some outburst of madness because of the limiting defects inherent in our species.

If there is any literary precedent for the image of man contained in Golding's fable, it is obviously not to be discovered within the framework of a tradition that embraces *Robinson Crusoe* and *Swiss Family Robinson* [6] and that includes also the island episodes in Conrad's novels where we see the self-defeating skepticism of a Heyst or a Decoud serving only to demonstrate the value of illusions.[7] All of these novels offer some version of the rationalist orthodoxy we so readily accept, even though the text may not be so boldly simple as Ballantyne's fable for innocent Victorians.

5. *Ulysses* (New York, 1961), p. 34.

6. Golding comments on these novels and on *Treasure Island* in his review called "Islands," *Spectator*, CCIV (June 10, 1960), pp. 844–46.

7. Most of the attempts to compare Golding with Conrad have been unsuccessful, but continued effort might bear some small fruit. At Purdue, Golding was asked by James Keating whether he had read Hughes's *High Wind in Jamaica* before writing *Lord of the Flies:* "No," he replied, "and if you're going to come around to Conrad's *Heart of Darkness,* I might as well confess that I've never read that."

Quite removed from this tradition (which Golding mocks in nearly everything he has written) is the directly acknowledged influence of classical Greek literature. Within this designation, though Golding's critics have ignored it, is the acknowledged admiration for Euripides.[8] Among the plays of Euripides it is *The Bacchae* that Golding, like his Mamillius of *The Brass Butterfly,* obviously knows by heart. The tragedy is a bitter allegory on the degeneration of society, and it contains a basic parable which informed much of Golding's work. It is clearly pertinent in *Lord of the Flies,* for here the point of view is similar to that of Euripides after he was driven into exile from Athens. Before his departure the tragedian brought down upon himself the mockery and disfavor of a mediocre regime like the one which later condemned Socrates. *The Bacchae,* however, is more than an expression of disillusionment with a failing democracy. Its aim is precisely what Golding has declared to be his own: "to trace the defects of society back to the defects of human nature," and so to account for the failure of rational man who invariably undertakes the blind ritual-hunt in which he seeks to kill the threatening "beast" within his own being.

The Bacchae is based on a legend of Dionysus wherein the god (a son of Zeus and the mortal Semele, daughter of Cadmus) descends upon Thebes in great wrath, determined to take revenge upon the young king, Pentheus, who has denied him recognition and prohibited his worship. Dionysus wins the daughters of Cadmus as his devotees; and, through his power of enchantment, he decrees that Agave, mother of Pentheus, shall lead the group in frenzied celebrations. Pentheus bluntly opposes the god and tries by every means to preserve order against the rising tide of

8. On every possible occasion Golding has noted his reading in Greek literature and history during the last twenty years. He reads in the original.

madness in his kingdom. The folly of his proud resistance is shown in the total defeat of all his efforts: the bacchantes trample on his rules and edicts; in wild marches through the land they wreck everything in their path. Thus prepared for his vengeance, Dionysus casts a spell over Pentheus. With his judgment weakened and his identity obscured by dressing as a woman, the humiliated prince sets out to spy upon the orgies. In the excitement of their rituals the bacchantes live in a world of illusion, and all that falls within their sight undergoes a metamorphosis which brings it into accord with the natural images of their worship. When Pentheus is seen, he is taken for a lion.[9] Led by Agave, the blind victims of the god tear the king limb from limb. The final punishment of those who denied the god of nature is to render them conscious of their awful crimes and to cast them out from their homeland as guilt-stricken exiles and wanderers upon the earth.

For most modern readers the chief obstacle in the way of proper understanding of *The Bacchae,* and therefore of Golding's use of it, is the popular notion that Dionysus is nothing more than a charming god of wine. This image descends from "the Alexandrines, and above all the Romans—with their tidy functionalism and their cheerful obtuseness in all matters of the spirit—who departmentalized Dionysus as 'jolly Bacchus' . . . with his riotous crew of nymphs and satyrs. As such he was taken over from the Romans by Renaissance painters and poets; and it was they in turn who shaped the image in which the modern world pictures him." In reality the god was more important and "much more dangerous": he was "the principle of animal life . . . the hunted and the hunter—the unrestrained potency which man envies in the beasts and seeks to assimilate." Thus the intention and chief effect of the

9. In Ovid's version (*Metamorphoses,* III), the bacchantes see Pentheus in the form of a boar.

bacchanal is "to liberate the instinctive life in man from the bondage imposed upon it by reason and social custom. . . ." In his tragedy Euripides also suggests "a further effect, a merging of the individual consciousness in a group consciousness" so that the participant is "at one not only with the Master of Life but his fellow-worshippers . . . and with the life of the earth." [10]

Dionysus was worshiped in various animal incarnations (snake, bull, lion, boar), whatever form was appropriate to place; and all of these incarnations were symbolic of the impulses he evoked in his worshipers. In *The Bacchae* a leader of the bacchanal summons him with the incantation, "O God, Beast, Mystery, come!" [11] Agave's attack upon the "lion" (her own son) conforms to the codes of Dionysic ritual: like other gods, this one is slain and devoured, his devotees sustained by his flesh and blood. The terrible error of the bacchantes is a punishment brought upon the proud Greeks by the lord of beasts: "To resist Dionysus is to repress the elemental in one's own nature; the punishment is the sudden collapse of the inward dykes when the elemental breaks through perforce and civilization vanishes." [12]

This same lesson in humility is meted out to the schoolboys of *Lord of the Flies*. In their innocent pride they attempt to impose a rational order or pattern upon the vital chaos of their own nature, and so they commit the error and "sin" of Pentheus, the "man of many sorrows." The penalties (as in the play) are bloodshed, guilt, utter defeat of reason. Finally, they stand before the officer, "A semicircle of little boys, their bodies streaked with colored clay, sharp

10. E. R. Dodds, *Euripides Bacchae,* Second Edition (Oxford, 1960), p. xii and p. xx. Dodds also finds evidence that some Dionysian rites involved human sacrifice.
11. From the verse translation by Gilbert Murray.
12. Dodds, p. xvi.

sticks in their hands. . . ." (pp. 240–41) Facing that pur-blind commander (with his revolver and peaked cap), Ralph cries "for the end of innocence, the darkness of man's heart" (p. 242); and the tribe of vicious hunters joins him in spontaneous choral lament. But even Ralph could not trace the arc of their descent, could not explain why it's no go, why things are as they are. For in the course of events he was at times among the hunters, one of them; and he grieves in part for the appalling ambiguities he has discovered in his own being. In this moment of "tragic knowledge" he re-members those strange interims of blindness and despair when a "shutter" clicked down over his mind and left him at the mercy of his own dark heart. In Ralph's experience, then, the essence of the fable is spelled out: he suffers the dialectic we must all endure, and his failure to resolve it as we would wish demonstrates the limitations which have always plagued our species.

In the first hours on the island Ralph sports untroubled in the twilight of childhood and innocence, but after he sounds the conch he must confront the forces he has sum-moned to the granite platform beside the sunny lagoon. During that first assembly he seems to arbitrate with the grace of a young god (his natural bearing is dignified, princely); and, for the time being, a balance is maintained. The difficulties begin with the dream revelation of the child distinguished by the birthmark. The boy tells of a snakelike monster prowling the woods by night, and at this moment the seed of fear is planted. Out of it will grow the mythic beast destined to become lord of the island. There is a plague of haunting dreams, and these constitute the first symptoms of the irrational fear which is "mankind's essen-tial illness."

In the chapter entitled "Beast from Water" the parlia-mentary debate becomes a blatant allegory in which each spokesman caricatures the position he defends. Piggy (the voice of reason) leads with the statement that "life is scientific," and adds the usual utopian promises ("when the war's over they'll be traveling to Mars and back"); and his assurance that such things will come to pass if only we control the senseless conflicts which impede our progress. He is met with laughter and jeers (the crude multitude), and at this juncture a little one interrupts to declare that the beast (ubiquitous evil) comes out of the sea. Maurice interjects to voice the doubt which curses them all: "I don't believe in the beast of course. As Piggy says, life's scientific, but we don't know, do we? Not certainly. . . ." (p. 102) Then Simon (the inarticulate seer) rises to utter the truth in garbled, ineffective phrases: there *is* a beast, but "it's only us." As always, his saving words are misunderstood, and the prophet shrinks away in confusion. Amid the speculation that Simon means some kind of ghost, there is a silent show of hands for ghosts as Piggy breaks in with angry rhetorical questions: "What are we? Humans? Or animals? Or Savages?" (p. 105) Taking his cue, Jack (savagery *in excelsis*) leaps to his feet and leads all but the "three blind mice" (Ralph, Piggy, and Simon) into a mad jig of release down the darkening beach. The parliamentarians naïvely contrast their failure with the supposed efficiency of adults; and Ralph, in despair, asks for a sign from that ruined world.

In "Beast from Air" the sign, a dead man in a parachute, is sent down from the grownups, and the collapse of order foreshadowed in the allegorical parliament comes on with surprising speed. Ralph himself looks into the face of the enthroned tyrant on the mountain, and from that moment his young intelligence is crippled by fear. He confirms the reality of the beast, insuring Jack's spectacular rise to absolute power. Yet the ease with which Jack establishes his Dionysian regime is hardly unaccountable. From its very first appearance, the black-caped choir, vaguely evil in its military *esprit,* emerged ominously from a mirage and marched down upon the minority forces assembled on the platform. Except for Simon, pressed into service and out of step with the common rhythm, the choir is composed of servitors bound by the rituals and the mysteries of group consciousness. They share in that communion, and there is no real "conversion" or transfer of allegiance from good to evil when the chorus, ostensibly Christian, becomes the tribe of hunters. The god they serve inhabits their own being. If they turn with relief from the burdens and responsibilities of the platform, it is because they cannot transcend the limitations of their own nature. Even the parliamentary pool of intelligence must fail in the attempt to explain all that manifests itself in our turbulent hearts, and the assertion that life is ordered, "scientific," often appears mere bravado. It embodies the sin of pride and, inevitably, it evokes the great god which the rational man would like to deny.

It is Simon who witnesses his coming and hears his words of wrath. In the thick undergrowth of the forest the boy discovers a refuge from the war of words. His shelter of leaves is a place of contemplation, a sequestered temple scented and lighted by the white flowers of the night-blooming candle-nut tree. There, in secret, he meditates on the lucid but somehow oversimple logic of Piggy and Ralph and on the venal emotion of Jack's challenges to their authority. There, in the infernal glare of the afternoon sun, he sees the killing of the sow by the hunters and the erection of the pig's head on the sharpened stick. These acts signify not only the final release from the blood taboo but also obeisance to the mystery and god who has come to be lord of the island world. In the hours of one powerfully symbolic afternoon, Simon sees the perennial fall which is the central reality of our history: the defeat of reason and the release of Dionysian madness in souls wounded by fear.

Awed by the hideousness of the dripping head—an image of the hunters' own nature—the apprentice bacchantes suddenly run away; but Simon's gaze is "held by that ancient, inescapable recognition" (p. 165)—an incarnation of the beast or devil born again and again out of the human heart. Before he loses consciousness, the epileptic visionary "hears" the truth which is inaccessible to the illusion-bound rationalist and to the unconscious or irrational man alike. " 'Fancy thinking the Beast was something you could hunt and kill!' said the head. For a moment or two the forest and all the other dimly appreciated places echoed with the parody of laughter. 'You knew, didn't you? I'm part of you? Close, close, close! I'm the reason why it's no go? Why things are as they are?' " (p. 172) When Simon recovers from this trauma of revelation, he finds on the mountaintop that the "beast" is only a man. Like the pig itself, the dead man in the chute is fly-blown, corrupt; he is an obscene image of the evil that has triumphed in the adult world as well. Tenderly the boy releases the lines so that the body can descend to earth, but the fallen man does not descend. After Simon's death, when the truth is once more lost, the figure rises, moves over the terrified tribe on the beach, and finally out to sea—a tyrannous ghost (history itself) which haunts and curses every social order.

In his martyrdom Simon meets the fate of all saints. The truth he brings would set us free from the repetitious nightmare of history, but we are, by nature, incapable of perceiving that truth. Demented by fears our intelligence cannot control, we are "at once heroic and sick" (p. 121), ingenious and ingenuous at the same time. Inevitably we gather in tribal union and communion to hunt the molesting "beast," and always the intolerable frustration of the hunt ends as it must: within the enchanted circle formed by the searchers the beast materializes in the only form he can possibly assume, the very image of his creator. And once he is visible, projected (once the hunted has become the hunter), the circle closes in an agony of relief. Simon, the saintly one, is blessed and cursed by those unique intuitions which threaten the ritual of the tribe. In whatever culture he appears, the saint is doomed by his insights. There is a vital, if obvious, irony to be observed in the fact that the lost children of Golding's fable are of Christian heritage; but, when they blindly kill their savior, they reenact not only an ancient tragedy but a universal one because it has its true source in the defects of the species.

The beast, too, is as old as his maker and has assumed many names, though of course his character must remain quite consistent. The particular beast who speaks to Simon is much like his namesake, Beelzebub. A prince of demons of Assyrian or Hebrew descent, but later appropriated by Christians, he is a lord of flies, an idol for unclean beings. He is what all devils are: merely an embodiment of the lusts and cruelties which possess his worshipers and of peculiar power among the Philistines, the unenlightened, fearful herd. He shares some kinship with Dionysus, for his powers and effects are much the same. In *The Bacchae* Dionysus is shown "as the source of ecstasies and disasters, as the enemy of intellect and the defense of man against his isolation, as a power that can make him feel like a god while acting like a beast. . . ." As such, he is "a god whom all can recognize." [13]

Nor is it difficult to recognize the island on which Golding's innocents are set down as a natural paradise, an uncorrupted Eden offering all the lush abundance of the primal earth. But it is lost with the first rumors of the "snake-thing," because he is the ancient, inescapable presence who insures a repetition of the fall. If this fall from

13. R. P. Winnington-Ingram, *Euripides and Dionysus: An Interpretation of the Bacchae* (Cambridge, England; 1948), pp. 9–10.

grace is indeed the "perennial myth" that Golding explores in all his work,[14] it does not seem that he has found in Genesis a metaphor capable of illuminating the full range of his theme. In *The Bacchae* Golding the classicist found another version of the fall of man, and it is clearly more useful to him than its Biblical counterpart. For one thing, it makes it possible to avoid the comparatively narrow moral implications most of us are inclined to read into the warfare between Satan (unqualifiedly evil) and God (unqualifiedly good). Satan is a fallen angel seeking vengeance on the godhead, and we therefore think of him as an autonomous entity, as a force in his own right and as prince of his own domain. Dionysus, on the other hand, is a son of God (Zeus) and thus a manifestation of one aspect of the godhead or mystery with whom man seeks communion or, perverse in his rational pride, denies at his own peril. To resist Dionysus is to resist nature itself, and this attempt to transcend the laws of creation brings down upon us the punishment of the god. Further, the ritual hunt of *The Bacchae* provides something else not found in the Biblical account of the fall. The hunt on Golding's island emerges spontaneously out of childish play, but it comes to serve as a key to the psychology underlying adult conflicts and, of course, as an effective symbol for the bloody game we have played throughout our history. This is not to say that Biblical metaphor is unimportant in *Lord of the Flies,* or in the later works, but that it forms only a part of the larger mythic frame in which Golding sees the nature and destiny of man.

Unfortunately, the critics have concentrated all too much on Golding's debts to Christian sources, with the result that he is now popularly regarded as a rigid Christian moralist.

14. See Ian Gregor and Mark Kinkead-Weekes, "The Strange Case of Mr. Golding and His Critics," *Twentieth Century,* CLXVIII (February, 1960), p. 118.

This is a false image. The emphasis of the critics has obscured Golding's fundamental realism and made it difficult to recognize that he satirizes both the Christian and the rationalist point of view. In *Lord of the Flies,* for example, the much discussed last chapter offers none of the traditional comforts of Christian orthodoxy. A fable, by virtue of its far-reaching suggestions, touches upon a dimension that most fiction does not—the dimension of prophecy. With the appearance of the naval officer, it is no longer possible to accept the evolution of the island society as an isolated failure. The events we have witnessed constitute a picture of realities which obtain in the world at large. There, too, a legendary beast has emerged from the dark wood, come from the sea, or fallen from the sky; and men have gathered for the communion of the hunt.

In retrospect, the entire fable suggests a grim parallel with the prophecies of the Biblical Apocalypse. According to that vision, the weary repetition of human failure is assured by the birth of new devils for each generation of men. The first demon, who fathers all the others, falls from the heavens; the second is summoned from the sea to make war upon the saints and overcome them; the third, emerging from the earth itself, induces man to make and worship an image of the beast. It also ordains that this image shall speak and cause those who do not worship the beast to be killed. Each devil in turn lords over the earth for an era, and then the long nightmare of history is broken by the second coming and the divine millennium. In *Lord of the Flies* (note some of the chapter titles) we see much the same sequence, but it occurs in a highly accelerated evolution. The parallel ends, however, with the irony of Golding's climactic revelation. The childish hope of rescue perishes as the beast-man comes to the shore, for he bears in his nature the bitter promise that things will remain as they are—and as they have been since his first appearance ages and ages ago.

The rebirth of evil is made certain by the fatal defects inherent in human nature, and the haunted island we occupy must always be a fortress on which enchanted hunters pursue the beast. There is no rescue. The making of history and the making of myth are finally the selfsame process—an old one in which the soul makes its own place, its own reality.

In spite of its rich and varied metaphor *Lord of the Flies* is not a bookish fable, and Golding has warned that he will concede little or nothing to *The Golden Bough.*[15] There are grave dangers in ignoring this disclaimer. To do so is to ignore the experiential sources of Golding's art and to obscure its contemporary relevance. During the period of World War II, he witnessed at firsthand the expenditure of human ingenuity in the old ritual of war. As the illusions of his earlier Rationalism and Humanism fell away, new images emerged; and, as for Simon, a picture of "a human at once heroic and sick" formed in his mind. When the war ended, Golding was ready to write (as he had not been before), and it was only natural to find in the traditions he knew the metaphors which could define the continuity of the soul's ancient flaws. In one sense, the "fable" was already written. Golding had but to trace over the words upon the scroll [16] and so collaborate with history.

15. See Golding's reply to Professor Kermode in "The Meaning of it All," *Books and Bookmen,* V (October, 1959), p. 9.

16. In a letter to me (September, 1962) Professor Kermode cites Golding's remark to the effect that he was "tracing words already on the paper" during the writing of *Lord of the Flies.*

2 ‡ *The dark spring*

For the greater part of his life Golding has lived in a region of England where it is impossible to forget the past, the remote past; and quite early in his youth he became fascinated by the speculations and discoveries of archaeologists and anthropologists. In one personal essay [1] he speaks of his first ventures into the countryside in search of relics of ancient man. Where the later Roman roads converge on the broad plain of Salisbury, he explains, "there was a prehistoric metropolis and the cathedral of that metropolis was Stonehenge. The whole of this area is sown thick with the remains of ancient people. To spend your life here in Wessex, as I have done, is to live where archaeology is natural—or as usual as gardening." Thus Golding began to form in his mind a first dim picture of the inheritors of the earth.

This first picture was radically different from the unflattering image we see in his fable of prehistory, *The Inheritors,* for it took shape long before the disillusionments

1. "Digging for Pictures," *Holiday,* XXXIII (March, 1963), pp. 86–87 ff.

of the war years and the crucial encounter with Greek literature. The toppled remains at Stonehenge are not far from the great cathedral in Salisbury, its magnificent Gothic spire reaching four hundred feet into the sky. The two monuments, so closely juxtaposed in space, would now strike Golding as closer in time than he had imagined as a boy. They would suggest the spiritual kinship of ancient and modern man; the continuity of human isolation, longing, and fear; the potent imagination which has made us such ingenious mythmakers throughout our long and level history. In *The Inheritors* the victims of human illusion are Neanderthal cave men, a small band of innocent and utterly harmless creatures who are taken for beasts or devils and so promptly annihilated by the more "advanced" species. The latter is clearly our ancestor, because his behavior matches that of the frightened schoolboys of *Lord of the Flies*. Golding, therefore, implies that the long course of evolution has brought no fundamental change in human nature. We are today essentially what we were in the past —heroic and sick, enisled and afraid. Though we have inherited the earth, we remain hunters and ritualists, using our weapons and incantations with the same seriousness and blind conceit that possessed the first of our kind.

Both *Lord of the Flies* and *The Inheritors* attack the pride of modern man who fancies that he is a rational creature in control of his own destiny; and both employ the same device, the clash of two tribes, as a means of illustrating the folly and danger of this illusion. In a BBC radio interview with Golding, Professor Frank Kermode discovered still another point of likeness when he asked "whether there is anything in the genesis of *The Inheritors* comparable to the position that Ballantyne has in the development of *Lord of the Flies*." [2] The reply goes beyond

2. In "The Meaning of it All," *Books and Bookmen,* V (October, 1959), p. 10.

the immediate question and, indirectly, explains why the fables have a similar structure:

> Yes, there's the brash optimism that H. G. Wells exhibits in *The Outline of History*. . . . Wells' *Outline of History* played a great part in my life because my father was a rationalist, and the *Outline* . . . was something he took neat. Well now, Wells' *Outline of History* is the rationalist's gospel *in excelsis*, I should think. I got this from my father, and by and by it seemed to me not to be large enough. It seemed to me to be too neat and slick. And when I re-read it as an adult I came across his picture of Neanderthal man, our immediate predecessors, as being the gross brutal creatures who were possibly the basis of the mythological bad man, whatever he may be, the ogre. I thought to myself that this is just absurd. What we're doing is externalising our own inside.

This passage from Wells's chapter on Neanderthal man, reprinted in part as the epigraph for *The Inheritors,* provides the basis for Golding's plot or "fable." [3] Prehistoric men come upon a last remnant of the Neanderthal tribes, kill as many as they dare, then flee in terror from the region haunted by these hairy "devils," and they bear with them an indelible memory of the encounter with nightmare monsters. Golding's Neanderthals, in appearance, are the same gorillalike beings Wells described, but their nature is entirely different. They are no more like devils than the wild hunters of *Lord of the Flies,* in an inversion of another kind, resemble the sweet and reasonable lads of Ballantyne's *Coral Island.* The cave men are gentle in disposition, unbelievably innocent, and without the ability to perceive that the new men bear evil motives in their hearts. Wells's

---

3. See also Peter Green, "The World of William Golding," *Review of English Literature,* I (April, 1960), p. 67. Green points out that Golding also had in mind Wells's short story, "The Grisly Folk." Wells here portrays the Neanderthals as ugly monsters but easily outwitted by our ingenious ancestors.

"ogre," then, proves to be nothing more than another projection of the beast within the dark heart of man; he is a "mythological bad man," an incarnation of the demon which has always haunted our species.

For some readers this will seem quite unfair to Wells. They remember him for his studied objectivity, his steadfast atheism, and, finally, for the abysmal despair of his last book, *Mind at the End of Its Tether;* but the younger historian of the *Outline* tacitly accepts that familiar mystique in which the mere passage of time somehow adds to human refinement and accomplishment. This kind of optimism was common enough during the Victorian twilight, and Golding's attack is apparently directed against that entire generation which bequeathed to us so many Ballantyne-like illusions. Among them was the notion that the survival of a species attests to its fitness or superiority (an assumption which tends to overrate the platypus) and the comforting belief that our historical record, however jagged, is a perennial heroic epic.

It was this picture of man, or one very much like it, that Golding must have seen during those early days of archaeological adventure when he first read Wells and fell under the influence of his father's rationalism. In his witty (and neglected) autobiographical essay, "The Ladder and the Tree," [4] he describes his father's views as follows: "Science was busy clearing up the universe. There was no place in this exquisitely logical universe for the terrors of darkness. There was darkness, of course, but it was just darkness, the absence of light. . . . God might have been a help but we'd thrown Him out, along with Imperialism, Toryism, the Exploitation of Women, War, and the Church of England." Now, in order to join this march of progress,

4. *The Listener,* LXIII (March 24, 1960), pp. 531–33. The essay was first presented on a BBC Third Program (March 13th), produced by Owen Leeming.

one had to give up childish ways; one had to learn Latin and grow up to be a scientist:

> Rules, declensions, paradigms and vocabularies stretched before me. They were like a ladder which I knew now I should climb, rung after factual rung and Sir James Jeans and Professor Einstein were waiting at the top to sign me on. I was glad about science in a remote sort of way. If you were going to be anything, then a scientist was what you ought to be. But the ladder was so long. In this dreary mood of personal knowledge and prophecy I knew that I should climb it; knew too that the darkness was all around, inexplicable, unexorcised, haunted, a gulf across which the ladder lay without reaching to the light.

By the time Golding came to write *The Inheritors* these childhood forebodings had been confirmed in experience, and the image of man put forward by Ballantyne and Wells assumed its proper designation as storybook fancy. Wells, however, seems to be a little more than another straw man. *The Inheritors* flatly rejects his attitudes, but it utilizes a kind of Wellsian technique. In many of his romances and fantasies Wells examined human behavior from some outsider's point of view or from some remote station in time. Again and again the time machine provided a means of establishing a post of observation from which he could make an ostensibly objective analysis of human affairs or a prediction of things to come. A clever fantasist, Wells was also a sentimental idealist; he was convinced (until his last years) that the power of reason could transform man and the world. Our progress, though, was painfully slow; and, as if to urge us along the way, he often measured the present against the tantalizing magnificence of the future. In Golding's story this formula is reversed: we measure man and his future in terms of the Neanderthal and his past. Through the eyes of the doomed innocents, we witness the triumph of Homo sapiens, but in the final chapter Golding strikes his usual ironic blow. There is a sudden shift to the point of view of the "rational" men. Terrified by the hulking "devils" they have seen, the new men sail their boats far out on the waters of a vast lake. We enter the mind of Tuami, one of the tribal leaders, and find him rationalizing the murder of the innocents. From within the shadow of his own nature the primitive man looks out upon the world, and we know that the dark shapes he sees will haunt the future. There is no real escape, no rescue; man the mythmaker, the perpetual Wellsian fantasist, is doomed to suffer from the threats and horrors bred in his own dark heart.

For all but this final episode Golding is committed to the simple one-dimensional sensibility of *Homo primigenius,* the Neanderthal; and the progression of events must be rendered at the unambiguous level of a prelogical mentality. This unusual point of view is managed with great craft and consistency, and the end result is an amazing stylistic tour de force. But it is one which taxes the patience of readers who expect the more easily available excitements afforded by the traditional narrative method of *Lord of the Flies*. Inevitably, there is some obscurity because the childlike Neanderthals are bound to miscalculate the motives and misinterpret the behavior of the strange men. There are intervals in which the naïve level of perception fails to provide a clear image for the reader, but the confusion is never more than temporary. Whatever may be initially obscure ends in some unmistakable irony which serves to demonstrate the great rift between the two species. In one early encounter the innocent Lok watches as an invader shoots a poisoned arrow at him: "The man turned sideways in the bushes and looked at Lok along his shoulder. A stick rose upright and there was a lump of bone in the middle. . . . The stick began to grow shorter at both ends. Then it shot out to full length again." (p. 106)

Unaccustomed to this level of receptivity, we are tempted to dismiss the cave man as stupid, but such a judgment (common among the reviewers of the book) is inaccurate and highly dangerous as a basis for interpretation. It ignores entirely the distinction Golding so frequently draws between innocence and stupidity. All perception is conditioned by the perceiver. According to Golding, the reality we inhabit is only a synthetic "picture" or pattern which we compose according to the limitations of our nature. And the whole point is that both tribes are caught in their own illusions. Lok, a boyish innocent without a sense of evil, regards the arrow as a gift. The language which reports its coming (fresh and precise within its limits) plays off his error in interpretation against the equally foolish error of his assailant. In the course of the narrative Golding creates by this means an impressive catalogue of Neanderthal virtues, which includes, ironically, the entire list of what we would call "Christian" attributes. Thus, as we read the final chapter, it is hardly the bewilderment or stupidity of the Neanderthal that stands out but the nonhuman magnitude of his heart. His failure to survive proves only that the meek were not really fit to inherit the earth, and who, in his sapience, will find that a cause for celebration?

Yet the blame for extinction of the Neanderthals does not fall entirely upon the new men. Before the coming of the intelligent hunters, the gentle species had begun its decline. Mal, their aged leader, speaks of "the time when there had been many people," a time "when it was summer all year around and the flowers and fruit hung on the same branch." (p. 35) Though that golden age does not lie within the living memory of the old man, his tale, a perpetual source of delight for the tribe, shows that these people were once numerous and that their environment was more congenial to creatures of passive nature. Now they are only eight in number, incestuous, driven by the harsh new seasons between the damp winter cave by the sea (where Fa's infant died and Mal became ill) and the short-lived summer of the uplands. Thus the old man's story is not simply an Edenic legend. For a time, the mothering earth offered a garden world in which innocence could thrive; but, helpless in the throes of her own evolution, she no longer provides for the offspring of that perishing age. The Neanderthals, therefore, were doomed from the very beginning by their trust in the changing earth and their naïve faith in the benevolence of their goddess, Oa. If she once gave them fruit and flowers on the same branch, the steadfast sun of paradise, ultimately she would betray them by producing the radical seasons and the cunning, upright beasts.

The narrative begins on the eve of their fall, but to the unsuspecting Neanderthals the last springtime trek to the cave by the river seems only another occasion for "happiness and exultation." "Oa had waited for them. Even now she was pushing up spikes of the bulbs, fattening the grubs, reeking the smells out of the earth, bulging the fat buds out of every crevice and bough." (pp. 31–32) Oa, mother of all, fecundity itself, is worshiped for her generosity. She is the source from which all life descends: "She brought forth the earth from her belly. She gave suck. The earth brought forth woman and the woman brought forth the first man out of her belly." (p. 35) Since the female is of direct descent, the old woman of the tribe is guardian of Oa's greatest gifts, fire and food, and priestess of Oa's greatest mysteries, birth and death. A woman is the living image of Oa and the bearer of life. But she is only the agent of that mystery and she is entirely innocent: the joy of love is one gift, the coming of a "new one" another. Just as the making of a new life is the sacred prerogative of Oa, so is the power to take a life. The people do not spill the blood of animals. They have not invented an offensive weapon because they have known little fear or violence. Theirs is a heritage of abundance.

In the very first encounter between the two species, the innocent Neanderthal demonstrates that he is ill-prepared to survive the new age. When he spies one of the others he is both "frightened and glad." And, according to the dictates of his nature, he rushes forward in awe and joy. But Homo sapiens sees in this apelike monster the incarnation of his own dark fears, and he flees in terror. Pursued, he strikes out, and so kills the "beast." Both have acted upon the impulses inherent in their nature, and both have been deceived. Their errors are inevitable, for both are fated to project their own soul: the innocent one lives in a fool's paradise; the cunning new man in a fool's hell.

After the sighting of the devils, the invaders summon the resources of their most powerful tribal traditions—the art of war and the science of magic. From the safety of their island camp [5] they make raids upon the cave, kill all but two of the adults, and carry the children away as captives. Lok and Fa, the remaining innocents, spy down upon the enemy from the top of a giant tree that becomes for Fa, the female, a tree of bitter knowledge. She sees the strange men dress in the skins of stags to act out a ritual dance of the hunt; and she watches them draw magnificent pictures in the dust of the earth, magic images which reveal their heart's desire. Finally, in the drunken orgy of a night feast, she sees the many sins of a people possessed by lusts. With the burning of the Neanderthal child, Liku, and the eating of her flesh, cannibalism is added to the list of ugly traits which Wells had assigned to the wrong species.

This negative picture of human nature is modified some-

5. The island is an important symbol in all of Golding's works. It suggests the isolation of man in a frightening and mysterious cosmos, and the futility of his attempt to create an ordered preserve for himself in an otherwise patternless world.

what in the scenes that follow. When they attempt to rescue the Neanderthal infant, Lok and Fa inspire a new wave of terror. Under the stress of great fear, the humans move their heavy boats overland to the lake; and in this terrible portage they evidence their strength, their courage, and their genius. Looking upon these feats, Lok compares the new men with the most potent forces of his own world: " 'They are like the river and the fall . . . ; nothing stands against them.' " He recognizes in them the creative power of his god: " 'They are like Oa.' " (p. 195) But his high praise is countered by Fa, for she senses the fear beneath this pointless heroism: " 'The new people are frightened. . . . They heave and sweat and watch the forest over their backs. But there is no danger in the forest.' " (p. 206) It is not until after Fa's death that young Lok learns to perceive the truth for himself. While Fa lived, he had seen about her the mystery of Oa; and, because he deferred to her judgment, his own initiation into the reality of evil has been postponed. For the description of his last hours of life the narrative perspective shifts, and we seem to look down from some height upon the last discoveries of "the red creature" as he loses his innocence. When he grasps the fact that Oa has released upon the world a beast in his own image, he returns to the tribal cave. There, lying in the dust, he takes up the foetal burial position, inviting Oa to shelter him in her womb. As he dies, the rising sun strikes the snowy crowns of the mountains and the "ice women" that his people worship begin to melt and fall. Far out on the lake, where the more intelligent enemy has fled, the downfall of the old gods reverberates ominously, announcing the new season and the new age. In this dark spring, sapient man has inherited the earth.

Tuami sits at the tiller of the boat and contemplates the uncertain future. The encounter has somehow changed his people. They came to this region as "bold hunters and magicians," but now they are "haunted, bedevilled, full of strange irrational grief. . . ." (pp. 224–25) The lusty woman, Vivani, feeds at her breast the infant devil they have taken with them. It affords her a compensation for the still-born child she lost on the long journey to this nightmare land. She shudders with horror but offers her love, and all of the people share her emotion. They reach out to the little devil in ambivalent homage and laugh at his antics. Tuami is also uncertain and afraid. Around the shoreline of the unexplored lake the dark forest makes a "line of darkness," encircling the boat and all her enchanted souls. Tuami cannot see beyond that line, and in despair he gives up the sharpening of his knife. It seems a useless weapon against the measureless unknown, against the terror: " 'Who would sharpen a point against the darkness of the world?' " (p. 231) He looks out upon the now-contaminated earth, and his speculations foretell the trials to come during the reign of the new men. In the coming of age of reason, the ingenuity of his people will be called upon again and again as they struggle to rescue themselves from the gods and demons who will be born out of their own absurd genius.

Against the tragic gloom of this conclusion the "brash optimism" of Wells stands out in bold relief, and the equation of evolution with progress, implicit in his *Outline,* emerges as nothing more than a rationalization. The pattern he imposed upon history is one we are all inclined to accept, because it offers such a flattering picture of human nature: man appears as the captain of his own soul and as the master of the earth. *The Inheritors* is designed to counter this commonly held illusion, and in this respect it is similar not only to *Lord of the Flies* but to *Pincher Martin.* All three of the fables are alike in basic structure, Golding explains, "because I was trying to say to people, 'Now look, I have a view which you haven't got and I would like you to see this from my point of view. Therefore, I must first put it so graphically in my way of thinking that you identify yourself with it, and then at the end I'm going to put you where you are, looking at it from the outside.' " [6]

The method is not without its dangers and limitations, and in *The Inheritors* Golding comes up against some of the generic problems that have always hounded the art of fable. If the writer is to achieve a lucid personification of attitudes, and so establish the stable symbolism on which fable depends, the purity or autonomy of each point of view must be maintained. The vital tensions and dialectics which sustain narrative interest must arise between—but not within—representative characters or tribes. Unless this rule of thumb is observed, ironies will be diminished in force and the ultimate moral obscured or even lost. We find in *The Inheritors* the traits of each species frozen in a radical contrast which sustains the allegory but threatens the illusion of reality. This rigidity also obscures the fact that Golding is actually a very knowledgeable archaeologist.[7] The incredibly innocent Neanderthals have somehow remained totally blind to the indifference and neutrality of Oa, even though they have lived for generations among saber-toothed tigers and witnessed the assaults of fire and ice upon their waning earthly paradise. The new men, on the other hand, seem completely depraved: there is no wavering and uncommitted Ralph and no Simon; and their absence leaves things very dark indeed. In *Lord of the Flies* the psychological development of these two characters is vividly dramatized. Further, the decline of rationality among the hunters appears to grow quite naturally out of

6. In "The Meaning of it All," p. 10. (See note 2 above.)

7. Except for this point, *The Inheritors* demonstrates a sound knowledge of recent archaeological and anthropological literature, but it is difficult to trace some of Golding's details to specific sources.

the interchange between their inherent limitations and the pressures of a trying existential condition. In spite of the extreme and arbitrarily created situation of the castaways, the earlier book evokes the pity and terror of a tragic defeat. The second fable falls short of that dimension because there is no significant dialectic suffered by the protagonists. Lok's fall from innocence consists largely of a series of animal discoveries: he sniffs along the ground and finally puts together in his mind the pattern of horrors. His accomplishment is hardly to be compared with Ralph's final epiphany on the beach.

Golding is too well acquainted with the principles of classical tragedy to be unaware of the generic flaw that limits the art of fable: "the fabulist is always a moralist, he is always overstating his case because he has a point he wishes to drive home." [8] In *The Inheritors* the most vital point he tried to drive home is obscured, rather than illuminated, by the fabulist's exaggerations. The moral implications of the story overwhelm its philosophical significance, with the result that most readers, impressed by the evil nature of primitive man and the pathos of the Neanderthal's demise, fail to recognize that *both* tribes are caught in illusion. Both are finite creatures, and, like all things born to die, they are too small and weak to resist cosmic changes or to fathom the mysteries of an inexorable evolutionary process. Yet it is difficult to blame the reviewers for seeing in Golding's favorite among his fables little more than a rebuff of Wellsian optimism. In this narrower interpretation, the book is easily reduced to bluntly moralistic terms. Golding, framed as an allegorist and moralist, emerged as an unappealing figure for "advanced" moderns. The depth of the misunderstanding was not to become entirely clear

8. In the interview conducted by James Keating at Purdue University.

to him until after the publication of his third fable. The confusion that followed *Pincher Martin* demonstrated the breakdown in communication and the pressing need for an experiment in a new mode.

3 ‡ *The absurd heroism of fallen man*

The widespread controversy over *Pincher Martin* must have provided an ironic surprise for Golding. He had approached the writing of this book with special care and determination; above all, as he explained later, he had aimed for clarity of communication: "I would have said that I fell over backwards making that novel explicit. I said to myself, 'Now here is going to be a novel, it's going to be a blow on behalf of the ordinary universe, which I think on the whole to be the right one, and I'm going to write it so vividly and so accurately and with such an exact programme that nobody can possibly mistake what I mean.' " [1] The expected result did not follow. In the midst of the confusion among readers and critics, Golding, for all his pains, found himself designated "Britain's controversial novelist." When the book was published in America, the title was changed to *The Two Deaths of Christopher Martin*,[2] but this blatant hint had no effect. In our efforts to interpret Martin's adventure we fared no better than the

1. In "The Meaning of it All," *Books and Bookmen*, V (October, 1959), p. 10.
2. *The Two Deaths of Christopher Martin* (New York, 1956).

English, and Golding was faced with mounting evidence that his carefully planned novel had not been understood at all.

The plot, taken at the most superficial level, is simple enough. It turns on the old cliché of the drowning man who recalls the whole pattern of his life as he struggles for survival in the sea. Christopher Martin is a lieutenant in the Royal Navy. His destroyer is on convoy duty in the North Atlantic during World War II when it is struck by an enemy torpedo. Martin, flung from the bridge into the water, crawls up on a barren rock, and for seven days (or for what *seems* like seven days) he tries to keep himself alive in the hope of rescue. No rescue comes, and the desperate castaway is finally swept from the rock by a raging storm.

The difficulties in interpretation begin with the final chapter. As usual, the critics' debate centers on the abrupt shift in perspective and its impact on the narrative or "fable" which has come before. Seven days after Martin refuses "the selfless act of dying," his body is washed ashore on an island where it is recovered by Mr. Campbell. Appalled by "the sad harvest" of the long and weary war, he wonders if there is any surviving beyond the flesh. He puts this question to a naval officer, Mr. Davidson, whose job it is to recover the bodies of drowned men. But Davidson is a literal-minded man, a rationalist, and he fails to grasp the real import of Mr. Campbell's question:

> "If you're worried about Martin—whether he suffered or not—"
>
> .   .   .   .   .   .
>
> Mr. Campbell sighed.
> "Aye," he said, "I meant just that."
> "Then don't worry about him. You saw the body. He didn't even have time to kick off his seaboots." (p. 208)

Davidson, of course, is wrong—not about the boots but about the suffering. Like the naval officer at the end of *Lord of the Flies,* or Tuami in the concluding chapter of *The Inheritors,* Davidson fails to see that the soul insists upon making its own reality, both here and hereafter. His rational interpretation contradicts what is already firmly established by the narrative—that Christopher Martin suffered an excruciating ordeal on the rock—and the reader is immediately in trouble if he falls into Davidson's error. There is actually no "trick ending," as some of the critics charged, unless we reject Golding's most basic theme and choose to stand on the adequacy of the rationalist's interpretation of experience. If one insists upon a similar reading of the last chapter of *Lord of the Flies,* he is forced to conclude, with the naïve officer, that the boys on the island were engaged after all in nothing more than "fun and games"; and the innocent Neanderthals of *The Inheritors* must emerge as the evil beasts they were taken for by our rational ancestors. In *Pincher Martin* Golding employs the same device and the same structure he used to good effect in the earlier fables, and there is no valid reason for treating the third book as an exception.

Most of the critics, however, did not see this common design. The result was that they created a number of spurious problems which obscured Golding's book and contributed to the impression that his ability to communicate had fallen off sharply since *Lord of the Flies.* The academic scholars hoped to find a key to *Pincher Martin* by tracking down a literary source for the plot, but none of the parallels they uncovered proved as useful as the revelation of Ballantyne's influence on *Lord of the Flies* or Wells's part in the shaping of *The Inheritors.*[3] The true

3. Wayland Young, "Letter from London," *Kenyon Review,* XIX (Summer, 1957), pp. 477–78, points out that the rock on which Martin is stranded is Rockall, "a nearly vertical jagged tooth

source may lie in Golding's own wartime experiences, possibly in a kind of private nightmare he inherited from his years at sea, for his own statement about the novel says nothing at all about literary influences. In 1958, on the eve of a BBC radio production of the story, he offered a few words of explanation [4] which are far more helpful than anything in the critical literature. There would be no insult or injury to his art if this "mental lifeline," as he called it, should be reprinted in subsequent editions of *Pincher Martin:*

> Christopher Hadley Martin had no belief in anything but the importance of his own life; no love, no God. Because he was created in the image of God he had a freedom of choice which he used to centre the world on himself. He did not believe in purgatory and therefore when he died it was not presented to him in overtly theological terms. The greed for life which had been the mainspring of his nature, forced him to refuse the selfless act of dying. He continued to exist in a world composed of his own murderous nature. His drowned body lies rolling in the Atlantic but the ravenous ego invents a rock for him to endure on. It is the memory of an aching tooth. Ostensibly and rationally he is a survivor from a torpedoed destroyer: but deep down he knows

---

of rock sticking seventy feet up out of the North Atlantic, 200 miles from the nearest land, the island of St. Kilda"; Edwin Morgan, *"Pincher Martin* and the *Coral Island," Notes and Queries,* VII (April, 1960), p. 150, notes a passage in *Coral Island* in which the boy castaways conjecture that the captain of their ship probably survived the storm because they last saw him removing his seaboots as he struggled in the water; Peter Green, "The World of William Golding," *Review of English Literature,* I (April, 1960), p. 69, believes the source for Martin's situation is Michael Roberts's poem "Rockall": see Roberts' *Collected Poems* (London, 1958); Ian Blake, *"Pincher Martin:* William Golding and Taffrail," *Notes and Queries,* IX (August, 1962), pp. 309–10, feels that Golding must have been influenced by an episode in H. P. Dorling's *Pincher Martin, O. D.* (1916).

4. *"Pincher Martin," Radio Times,* CXXXVIII (March 21, 1958), p. 8.

the truth. He is not fighting for bodily survival but for his continuing identity in the face of what will smash it and sweep it away—the black lightning, the compassion of God. For Christopher, the Christ-bearer, has become Pincher Martin who is little but greed. Just to be Pincher is purgatory; to be Pincher for eternity is hell.

This explanation exposes in advance what is withheld in the narrative until the very last sentence—the fact that the entire struggle for survival on the rock takes place after the bodily death (the first death) of Pincher Martin. Armed with this foreknowledge, the reader discovers more readily the truth he is expected to find anyway. He sees, for example, that Martin really drowns shortly after he is thrown from the bridge of his ship by the blast of the torpedo. The floundering man hears the turbines of the destroyer screaming in his ears and "green sparks" fly out "from the centre [of his consciousness] like tracer. There was a piston engine too, racing out of gear and making the whole universe shake. Then for a moment there was air like a cold mask against his face and he bit into it. Air and water mixed, dragged down his body like gravel. Muscles, nerves, and blood, struggling lungs, a machine in the head, they worked for one moment in an ancient pattern." (pp. 7–8) With his last breath the man calls on his mother, but then his heavy seaboots pull him down and the adventure in the afterlife begins. This first death (it happens on the second page) is relatively unimportant, and there is no interruption in the narrative, no explicit announcement, because Pincher's ego does not capitulate at this point. His soul maintains its autonomy and continues to defy the darkness from which it was born but fears to return. In his sea dream Pincher Martin removes his seaboots, inflates his lifebelt, and goes on living in a world spun out of his own sick soul.

The critics who accepted Davidson's interpretation of Martin's fate were confronted with a problem of time, and this formed the mainstay for more than one exploratory essay.[5] The man could not have suffered, they reasoned, if he drowned before he had time to remove his boots; or, alternatively, the struggle which seemed prolonged and excruciatingly real was only a last flash of consciousness before Martin was put out of his misery. In either case, the ordeal was not as bad as it appeared to be, and Golding could be charged with pulling a "trick" on the unsuspecting reader. Such a conclusion is possible only if one denies the reality of all that lies beyond the visible evidence of the senses, as Davidson does, and so leaves out of account the mythopoeic genius of the human soul. As for the duration of Pincher's agony, the only valid measure of time is the experience itself: in the afterlife his egotistical soul usurps the role of creator; out of the formless void and darkness it makes anew both world and time. The desperate man clinging to the rock of his own ego parodies the acts of creation recorded in Genesis, he plays God; and his task requires the original seven days. Floating in the darkness on the face of the deep, he first creates light, distinguishes night and day so that the familiar cycle may continue, and then he invents a dry land or earth (the rock) which he endows with living creatures out of his stock of ugly memories.

5. See, e. g., Wayland Young (note 3 above) and James Gindin, "'Gimmick' and Metaphor in the Novels of William Golding," *Modern Fiction Studies,* VI (Summer, 1960), pp. 145–52. Gindin argues that Golding's metaphors "suggest the reality, the permanence, of the traditional Christian explanation of the nature of man" but that the "gimmick endings" contradict and limit the established import of these metaphors. Actually, the situation is exactly the reverse: the final chapters *intentionally* contradict the reality shown in the narrative—and thus expose the fallibility of the rational point of view. Further, the metaphors are drawn from classical as well as Christian sources, and one must take into account the classical allusions before attempting to derive Golding's real intention.

If this definitive metaphor is rather faintly sketched in the early chapters, it eventually comes across with unmistakable clarity. On the sixth "day," when his strength is nearly gone, Pincher achieves the final stroke: he creates God in his own image. The hallucination appears, dressed in an oilskin and (significantly) in seaboots, and the beleaguered ego of the man tries to dismiss it as a projection only, the effect of the ordeal it has endured. Addressing the image, Martin says: "On the sixth day he created God. Therefore I permit you to use nothing but my own vocabulary. In his own image he created Him." In the dialogue that follows, the castaway boasts: "I have created you and I can create my own heaven." And the figure then utters the truth which Pincher already knows deep in his heart: "You have created it." (p. 196) On the blessed seventh day, however, the weary creator finds rest from his labors. In what seems to him a violent storm, he is struck by the "black lightning" and swept off his rock. Through the "compassion" of God, the second death, Christopher Martin is rescued from his self-created nightmare.

The Biblical metaphor is really a key to *Pincher Martin,* and it is surely what Golding had in mind when he told Frank Kermode that he "fell over backwards" making the book explicit. The critics who missed the vital comparison failed on several counts: first, they raised the spurious problem of time; second, overlooking the colossal ironies that emerge out of Pincher's pride-blown insistence upon playing the role of God, they made a hero out of Golding's villain; finally, they put forward the misleading conclusion that Golding himself was moving directly into line with the contemporary existentialists. In the radio interview with Professor Kermode,[6] Golding tried to unravel the confusion:

6. "The Meaning of it All." (See note 1 above.)

GOLDING: My point is really this you see: that you meet a Christian—he thinks that when he dies he will either have devils with three-pronged forks and forked tails or angels with wings and palms. If you're not a Christian and die, then if the universe is as the Christian sees it, you will still go either to heaven or hell or purgatory. But your purgatory, or your heaven or your hell won't have the Christian attributes.

KERMODE: No, they'll be the things you make yourself.

GOLDING: They'll be the things you make yourself, and that's all there is to it. And that Pincher was a pincher. He'd spent the whole of his life acquiring things that really belonged to other people, and bit by bit they were taken away from him in purgatory, till he ended as what he was.

The struggle on the rock, Kermode points out, is of mythical proportion in that Martin, an arch sinner, represents "fallen man":

GOLDING: Very much fallen—he's fallen more than most. In fact, I went out of my way to damn Pincher as much as I could by making him the nastiest type I could think of, and I was very interested to see how critics all over the place said, "Well yes, we are like that."

In the course of the same interview Golding touched on a point which may explain at least one of the causes for this gross misinterpretation of *Pincher Martin:* "I think that my novels have very little genesis outside myself; that to a large extent I have cut myself off from contemporary literary life, and gained in one sense by it though I may have lost in another." Whatever the gain, one loss incurred in such alienation is misreading at the hands of those who have been conditioned by the literature of their time. Some of the critics were bound to see in Martin's lonely struggle for survival a kind of existential fable. Obviously, they did not see the relationship between the two levels of time, past and present; and, failing to see that the fragments of the past recalled on the rock expose a despicable moral history, they also failed to accept Pincher's agonies as morally justified. Martin, a satanic type, prefers to reign in his own hellish world rather than acknowledge a power beyond and above the limits of his own nature. If one does not perceive that his suffering is self-imposed, the fallen man appears in quite another light and the moral of the story is entirely reversed. Martin's strength of will, his uncanny ingenuity, and his martyr's capacity for enduring the slings and arrows of gross misfortune make of him an admirable existential hero who fights with great courage against the odds unjustly imposed upon him by an indifferent nature and an implacable deity. The attempt to read the book in the light of existentialist attitudes, however, erases the essential ironies Golding went out of his way to inject; and, if these are taken away, the theme is hopelessly obscured. Perverse in the extreme, Christopher Martin's soul tries to survive on its own terms, and it pays for this conceit by perpetuating the misery it knew in life. Finally, it must be rescued forcibly by an apparently cruel but actually compassionate God. Pincher's "heroism," therefore, is fundamentally absurd, and so the fable ends by inverting the existential formula certain of the critics wished to impose upon it. Instead of depicting the assault of reality on the hapless soul of rational man, Golding shows the outrageous attack of a rational man, who is far more sick than heroic, upon nature and God.[7]

7. But see Frederick Karl, "The Novel as Moral Allegory," in his *The Contemporary English Novel* (New York, 1962), pp. 254–55. Golding is again linked with existentialism in Margaret Walters' "Two Fabulists: Golding and Camus," *Melbourne Critical Review*, No. 4 (1961), pp. 18–19. These comparisons with the existentialists, like the parallels with Conrad, are not very convincing. Further scholarly effort is needed, but it is likely to end by tracing the relationships between Greek tragedy and modern existentialism.

Martin's understanding of his own spiritual development is necessarily hazy and incomplete, for a man so
deeply involved in the sin of pride does not recognize, let
alone concede, the errors through which he incurred a
burden of guilt. Thus it is a trying job to piece together
the scattered fragments from this personal history and to
discover when and how he fell from innocence and entered
into the ways that bring him to the purgatorial ordeal. It is
on this point, and not on the issues raised by the critics,
that communication nearly breaks down. We know that at
some time in the course of his earthly existence Christopher Martin, the "Christ-bearer" born in the image of
God, became the ugly being we find clinging to the rock,
but in every one of the flashbacks we find him, an actor by
profession, playing the role of one or another of the seven
deadly sins. Pride, of course, is the basic mortal flaw that
gives him such versatility. According to his director, Martin can take the part of covetousness, lust, anger, gluttony,
envy, or sloth, and play these "without a mask." But it is
difficult to account for his moral evolution, to trace things
back to the beginning, because the "pictures" which come
to his mind on the rock recur in no particular order. They
are like "an album of snapshots, random, a whole show
of trailers of old films" (p. 133), and only very gradually
does the reader establish even a rough chronology for the
man's development.

There are several moments of vision in which Martin
seems to realize that his present suffering is somehow related to the persistent waking nightmare he experienced as
a child,[8] and this insight is far more important than it
appears to be in the long tissue of memories. It illustrates
again Golding's thesis that fear is "mankind's essential ill-

8. Compare Golding's own childhood experiences, as related in
"The Ladder and the Tree," and the nightmares of Sammy Mountjoy in *Free Fall*.

ness" and his belief that our ethical nature is formed in the struggle between our inadequate rational faculty and the dark, inexorable heart. Inevitably, therefore, the process begins in the formative years of childhood:

> It's like those nights when I was a kid, lying awake thinking the darkness would go on forever. And I couldn't go back to sleep because of the dream of the whatever it was in the cellar coming out of the corner. I'd lie in the hot, rumpled bed, hot burning hot, trying to shut myself away and know that there were three eternities before the dawn. Everything was the night world, the other world where everything but good could happen, the world of ghosts and robbers and horrors, of things harmless in the daytime coming to life, the wardrobe, the picture in the book, the story, coffins, corpses, vampires, and always squeezing, tormenting darkness, smoke thick. And I'd think anything because if I didn't go on thinking I'd remember whatever it was in the cellar down there, and my mind would go walking away from my body and go down three stories defenseless, down the dark stairs past the tall haunted clock, through the whining door, down the terrible steps to where the coffin ends were crushed in the walls of the cellar—and I'd be helpless on the stone floor, trying to run back, run away, climb up— (p. 138)

The man on the rock knows in his heart there is a connection between his present nightmare and the microcosmic hell of the cellar, for he is still terrified by the darkness. The child endowed the underworld of the cellar with Gothic horrors and some nameless antagonist who threatened his very existence. The adult (like the little boys of *Lord of the Flies*) is mastered by the primal fear of the unknown; he projects his own image onto the antagonist (as the primitive men of *The Inheritors* did); and so he fears that the antagonist will be cruel and rapacious. No wonder his soul fights against the descent into darkness and death. He clings to the rock of his own ego—his own identity—to escape what his friend Nathaniel called "the black lightning," and his only defense is to go on thinking.

Just how do the fears of the boy lead to the gross sins, the "fall," of the adult? It is not easy to trace this line of development through Martin's disorganized memories because they are not put into chronological order and because there are some missing links in the pattern. His moral evolution, however, has something in common with that of other Golding characters, particularly Sammy Mountjoy of *Free Fall*. In order to avoid the terrors of the irrational, one must deny the irrational itself; one must deny the reality of all that he cannot comprehend and master. The "rational" man, therefore, imposes his own laws on the universe so that it will conform to his own sense of order and confirm his own logic. Such a man is no longer "innocent," for he pits his own will and intelligence against the patternlessness of a cosmos he cannot possibly control. His proud claim to knowledge and power leads him inevitably into temptation: he becomes a manipulator, a "pincher" or thief, intent on his own advantage; and his will and intelligence become merely limbs or claws to serve his ravenous ego.

Martin, of course, is so addicted to the sin of pride that he is incapable of seeing himself as the hideous creature he has become. In moments of rage and self-pity he feels he is the victim of a "bloody great bully," and he casts himself into the role of one or another of the mythical heroes who nobly opposed the injustice of a tyrannous god. He feels the weight of the arching sky on his shoulders and fancies himself Atlas; but in reality the burden he bears is self-created and lies compacted in the bone "globe" of his own skull. At other times he plays Prometheus and swears he will suffer for eternity rather than submit to the cruel wrong imposed upon him; but in reality he is chained only to the rock of his own proud ego. All of his tasks and punishments stem from his vain pride and intransigent greed for life. By virtue of his own persistence, Pincher ends as what he has made of himself—a pair of grasping claws.

The basic and structural metaphor in *Pincher Martin* depends upon the account of the Creation in the Book of Genesis; and the central irony of the fable becomes clear enough as soon as we see that Martin, representing human pride and greed, insists upon playing the role of the Biblical magician. With the injection of the Atlas and Prometheus comparisons, however, coupled with the final Ovidian metamorphosis, it becomes impossible to sum up the moral and metaphysical implications of the story in purely Christian terms. In fact, the closing scene of *Pincher Martin* demonstrates more clearly than any of the other works that Golding is a classical rather than a Christian moralist. The parallel for Martin's transformation into a pair of grasping claws is to be found in *The Metamorphoses*. In each of the tales recounted by Ovid a mortal, or an inferior deity of the earth, undergoes a bodily change: Arachne becomes a spider, Niobe a marble statue, and Hyacinthus a flower. The dehumanization of the subject represents either a blessing or a punishment ordained by one of the gods, and the particular physical change reflects an appropriate moral judgment. The new natural form assumed by the protagonist is invariably a fitting symbol or memorial for the cardinal sin or virtue he expressed in his earthly life. Golding makes use of both the positive and the negative moral fables contained in *The Metamorphoses*. His grasping Pincher ends "as what he was," but the sea change that befalls Simon after his death carries the opposite moral import. The saintly boy of *Lord of the Flies* is beatified or glorified as his body lies rolling in the phosphorus-infested waters of the surf. The luminous water forms a halo around his head, his face is gradually "silvered," and "the turn of his shoulder [becomes] sculptured marble." (p. 184)

Even an amateur classicist knows that Ovid is not simply a moralist. "Change is my theme," he announces, and then comes the long series of fables illustrating the mutability of all things in nature and the subtle relationships between spirit and matter expressed in these changes. The theoretical basis for the entire work is reviewed in Book XV. There Ovid provides a summary of the philosophy of his master, Pythagoras, giving special emphasis to the Orphic doctrine of metempsychosis. Golding, like Ovid, is much more than the moralist his critics have taken him to be, and there is no question that the metaphysical significance of his fables remains largely unexplored. To what extent it might be understood in the light of Ovid's archaeology and cosmology is difficult to guess, but it surely merits the attention of informed classical scholars. Meanwhile, there is no risk in asserting that Golding's beleaguered castaways suffer and die in a universe which is more pagan than Christian. If most of the critics have overlooked this fact, it is hardly fair to condemn them. One extenuating factor is that classical and Christian morality often converge and agree. The second is that Golding draws upon both traditions in an effort to define the realities of his cosmos, and the critics, naturally, concentrate on the more obvious and familiar metaphors which they inevitably associate with orthodox Christian thought.

In *Pincher Martin,* for example, there are at least two major difficulties and distractions put in the way of the average reader. He is first confronted with the structural metaphor taken from the Book of Genesis; and, even more confusing, there is the misleading impression he is almost bound to carry away from the account of Pincher's death, the first death. Golding's fallen man is struck down at the very moment he attempts the greatest crime of his career, the murder of his Christ-like friend, Nathaniel Walterson. As he gives the order calculated to throw Nathaniel from the railing of the destroyer into the sea, he hears simultaneously the blast of the enemy torpedo. It is an unexpected "destroying concussion that had no part in the play," no part in his evil plans, and for Martin there is no particular meaning to be read into the coincidence. Struggling in the icy water, he puts it down to his characteristic bad luck and reflects that if he had given the order a moment sooner he might have saved the ship and been decorated as a hero. The reader, who is not as cynical and depraved as Martin, cannot dismiss the coincidence so lightly. The explosion seems to announce the intrusion of some moralistic agent or cosmic force which objects to the evil little "play" projected in Pincher's mind. Unfortunately, it is likely to suggest the existence of a Jehovah-like deity who, at this point, reaches the limits of his patience with Christopher Martin's most audacious transgression of divine law.

There is no evidence that Golding believes in such a creature. The coincidence signifies that the plans and patterns conceived by rational minds, whether these minds be good or evil, are subject to bombardment and unpredictable change in a universe which is too large and mysterious to be controlled or contained by mortal desire and finite logic. This is not to say that such explosions are without moral significance; but here, as elsewhere, Golding offers no explicit image of a deity whose interference in our petty designs might hint of a cosmic order or law. Thus Golding became the victim of his own ambiguous metaphors, and the critics found enough latitude in his carefully planned novel to frame him once again as an orthodox moralist, writing in his obscure way of the justice of an enduring Christian God. It was with the intention of modifying this picture of himself, and in the hope of communicating the vital point that *Pincher Martin* and the other fables had failed to communicate, that he undertook a radically new approach in *Free Fall*. Frustrated by the misinterpretation he had endured for more than five years, he determined to merge theme and form in an effort to demonstrate the patternlessness or chaos in which men are fated to live.

4 ‡ History as comedy

The writing of a novel is a task Golding regards with "terrible seriousness," but his plays [1] are written in a spirit of fun and largely as a means of amusing himself. This was evidently the chief motivation behind his three-act comedy, *The Brass Butterfly,* and the *novella* "Envoy Extraordinary" on which it is based. "The story was written first," Golding explains, "and then when Alastair Sim asked me to write a play for him, always being a great believer in economy of means, I said, 'Well, here's a story which would make a play,' and I had fun writing it. It's a very imperfect play, but I enjoyed it nonetheless." [2] *The Brass Butterfly* was produced for the first time at the New Theatre in Oxford early in 1958; and, after some mild success there, it was again staged in London. With Sim in the role of Caesar, the protagonist, the play was bound to evoke

1. *The Brass Butterfly* is Golding's only published play. He has also written a drama called *Break My Heart,* produced as a BBC Radio Feature Program in 1962.
2. Golding's reply to James Keating in the interview held at Purdue University.

interest. Judging from the reviews,[3] however, its point did not come across clearly and audiences left the theater somewhat bewildered. Actually, both the story and the play repeat some of Golding's characteristic themes in a farcical manner. The "imperfect" little comedy is the most difficult to grasp. It is simply too economical, too compact; and, like everything else Golding has written, it is burdened with philosophical implications alien to the modern temper.

One approach to the meaning of the play has been suggested by the English critic, Peter Green, who believes that the basic plot is borrowed from Richard Garnett's short story called "The Rewards of Industry." [4] In that ironic tale two sons of a poor mandarin go into the world to make their fortunes as inventors. One presents a Western emperor with a printing press and the other offers an explosive powder, but both of these devices are rejected as useless and the ingenious inventors are threatened with execution for upsetting the *status quo*. A third son, less industrious and seemingly without promise, introduces the West to the game of chess. He is richly rewarded for his great gift to civilization. The moral of the story is that men are nothing more than irrational children who always prefer amusement before valuable instruction or discovery.

The Brass Butterfly follows a similar line of development and, though Green does not mention other parallels, most of the prose fables collected in Garnett's *The Twilight of the Gods* (1888) would be certain to please Golding. The entire volume mocks the confident rationalism of the late nineteenth century. In the title story, and in others ("Truth and Her Companions" or "The Three Palaces"),

3. See, e.g., J. C. Trewin, *"The Brass Butterfly," Illustrated London News,* CCXXXII (May 3, 1958), p. 748.

4. See Peter Green, "The World of William Golding," *Review of English Literature,* I (April, 1960), p. 68.

Garnett shows that the gods men worship are projections of their own desires and that the historian can measure the spiritual integrity of any age according to the deities it invents and adores. While these same ideas appear in Golding's comedy, they also appear in the three novels he wrote before the play was conceived. The extent of Garnett's influence, therefore, remains a matter for further exploration. Whatever his importance, the elements of *The Brass Butterfly*—the allegorical method, the character types, and the basic theme—are all to be found in Golding's earlier work.

In Golding's farce, Caesar, a cynical Epicurean and ardent gastronome, has retired to the island of Capri to find respite from the wearisome grandeur of Rome. On this pleasure island his only real companion is young Mamillius, an illegitimate son who is spoiled, bored, uncommitted to any serious purpose, and entirely without administrative talent. Postumus, the legitimate son, is more in the Roman tradition: he is brutal and unimaginative, but he is an efficient militarist and official heir to the Empire. As the play opens Postumus is away from the island in pursuit of some Christians who have escaped in a boat secretly provided them by the weary Emperor, who is determined to have a few days of peace and quiet. His only official duty is to grant interviews to those who petition him, and Caesar inadvertently destroys the tranquility of his retreat when he admits a Greek inventor bearing dangerous gifts.

Phanocles, the Greek, is the familiar Golding rationalist and he is endowed with the usual conceits. He boasts that he can move easily in the world of substance and force because he credits the universe "with at least a lawyer's intelligence." According to his illusion, the cosmos is law-abiding and logical, "a giant mechanism," and of course he puts no stock at all in the Olympian gods or in the new

Christianity—"that contradictory mixture of hysterical beliefs." The true destiny of man, Phanocles maintains, is to
control the universe through the power of reason. He puts
before the Emperor plans for several devices: one is an
explosive missile; another, a speedy steamship. In the
course of explaining the principle of steam power, the
Greek mentions a savage tribe which prepares food by
means of a pressure cooker, and Caesar, who sees little
point in the missile or in the ship, is immediately aroused
by the potentials of the utensil. But it is not this alone
which induces him to appoint the ingenious Greek his
Director General of Experimental Studies. The inventor
is accompanied by his sister, Euphrosyne, and young
Mamillius is awakened to passion by her great beauty. The
girl is named after one of the Graces, Joy, but she has
lately become a Christian. The effect is to stifle all natural
joys. To protect her own chastity she has veiled her face
from the world and taken a vow of silence.

When Postumus learns through his spies that the island
has become the scene of strange activities, he returns with
his army to investigate. The first thing he notes is an
ominous change toward manly bearing in the love-inspired
Mamillius. Interpreting this as political ambition, Postumus
next becomes suspicious of Caesar's motive in financing
the experiments of Phanocles. Thus the comedy of errors
begins. After the steamship gets out of hand and chews up
a number of his boats, Postumus decides to place the entire company under arrest until the Emperor can be made
to hand over command of the Empire.

Faced with this crisis, Caesar retires to his palace to try
the pressure cooker. Phanocles, outraged by this nonsense
and by the countless interruptions of his work, protests the
irrationality of men: "I have asked from men nothing but
good will and common sense. Yet the Emperor of the world
is preoccupied in there, eating from a toy I would never

have thought worth making. And down there a fool's finger is on my own trigger [the missile]. We build on the expectations of man's goodness and the foundations collapse under us." (p. 55) As Caesar emerges from the palace, elated beyond measure by the new gastronomic delight, Phanocles confronts him with the vital question:

> PHANOCLES: Caesar, I conquered the universe, and yet the ants have defeated me. What is wrong with man?

> EMPEROR: Men. A steam ship, or anything powerful, in the hands of man, Phanocles, is like a sharp knife in the hands of a child. There is nothing wrong with the knife. There is nothing wrong with the steam ship. There is nothing wrong with man's intelligence. The trouble is his nature. (p. 58)

Something of the philosophical essence of the play is contained in this exchange, but the full extent of Golding's diagnosis of man remains to be seen in the irrational melee of the last act.

Postumus, in an outburst of paranoid rage, threatens to blow up the palace with the inventor's missile, and Caesar's frightened band decides upon prayer as a last resort. Euphrosyne reveals her secret faith when she insists that they address her Christian god, but largely as a matter of protocol all stand silent as the Emperor invokes Great Jupiter. At the very moment he begs the Lord of Lightning to destroy their enemies, a tremendous explosion rocks the island. Postumus has aimed the missile at the palace, but on firing the Talus-like projectile something goes wrong and his entire force is destroyed. Naturally, Caesar and Mamillius wish to credit Jupiter, while Euphrosyne praises her god for their release. At his command, she says, she walked in a trance to the missile and removed the arming device, the brass butterfly, so that the projectile would explode on the spot. Phanocles is delighted with this stroke of intelligence and calculation, but the others will not listen to him. The effect of the coincidence is too much: "You can tell me nothing more," Caesar retorts. "Where is all your logic when the gods take a hand?" (p. 71)

Mamillius chooses this inspiring moment to ask for the hand of Euphrosyne, and Caesar, dubious as he is about the political effects of this union, gives them his blessing. With Postumus dead, the Roman Empire will fall into the hands of the bastard son, who promptly announces that he will accept the Christian god of his bride. Shaken by the twilight of the old world and the old gods, the Emperor requests a few hours of quiet contemplation. He immediately recognizes that a far greater threat to the future lies in Phanocles. The Christian regime of Mamillius and Euphrosyne will have little effect on the social order, but the mad Greek proposes new machines and revolutionary ideas. He describes for his patron a printing press and a wild scheme for universal education which would make all men "free." Frightened by these proposals, the Emperor's last official act is to send the dangerous genius as Envoy Extraordinary on "a *slow* boat to China." Once Phanocles is out of the way, the brave new world he envisions will at least be delayed; and, for a time, the awful progress he has in mind will not befall the world. Men will continue to live in the old universe of gods and devils, of beauty and injustice, untroubled by the "ferment, fever, dislocation, disorder," and catastrophe which the Emperor attributes to the perverse intelligence of his island guest.

It is unlikely that *The Brass Butterfly* will ever be a popular success in the theater. Even if the original text should be rewritten for future productions, it would take very clever staging and unusually adept acting—all of the powers of the stage—to communicate the full humor and the full meaning of this farce. And very probably a more successful version would end by antagonizing audiences, for the play satirizes both the rationalist and the true believer. In Phanocles we see the folly of the rational man. The optimistic dream of a new order, in which all men will behave reasonably and in their best interests, is doomed by the irrationality inherent in our species. In all of the other stylized characters of the play, including the witty Caesar, we observe typical modes of rationalization which allow men to believe that the real flux and chaos of the universe may add up to some kind of meaningful pattern. The island, of course, is a microcosm, and the inane episode that occurs there reflects the essentials of human nature and the illogicality of human history.

The evolution of affairs on the island (and in this respect the play is like *Lord of the Flies*) certainly does not suggest the straight line of progress the rationalist tries to impose on historical development; nor does it suggest any of the rewards and punishments which the moralist or religious idealist would like to read into things. The ancient dialectic inherent in human nature, the perennial clash of reason and madness, is inevitably reflected in history. In *Lord of the Flies* Golding looks upon the result as tragedy; in the play he sees the effects of human illusions as pure comedy.

The Brass Butterfly affords still another example of Golding's philosophical realism, but the real spirit of his comedy remains obscure to most readers. The play simply could not overcome or contradict the solidly established critical convention which represented Golding as a Christian moralist.

5 ‡ *The translation of incoherence into incoherence*

Free Fall is at one and the same time the most engaging and the most difficult of Golding's works. It is impressive above all for the intensity and power of its language; it is disappointing because it fails to attain the structural perfection of the earlier fables. In the criticism one finds both extravagant praise and grumbling discontent: on the one hand, a tendency to regard the novel as Golding's finest achievement; on the other, a wistful backward look toward the comparatively lucid allegories. This time, in contrast with the muddle over *Pincher Martin,* the ambivalent critical response seems to reflect the actual qualities and limitations inherent in the novel itself. *Free Fall* is brilliant and obscure, a triumph in one respect, a failure in another.

In the summer of 1958 Golding explained to an interviewer [1] something of the plan behind the new effort then in progress. The basic problem of modern man, he said, is "learning to live fearlessly with the natural chaos of exist-

1. Golding's remarks were made in the course of an unpublished interview conducted by Owen Webster and sent to me by Mr. Charles Monteith of Faber and Faber.

ence, without forcing artificial patterns on it." Most of us, however, refuse to accept the inevitable flux of experience: "The orthodox Christian, the Marxist, the scientific humanist, and so on, all deny certain experiences because they cannot be fitted into the more or less rigid patterns by which life is made comprehensible to them." As a result, they lose touch with reality and live in a distorted, artificial world of their own making. They become unnatural and perverted creatures, dangerous to themselves and others; they are, in a sense, dead souls, for "the difference between being alive and being an inorganic substance is just this proliferation of experience, this absence of pattern." *Free Fall* would seek to expose the common error of modern man by illustrating the fundamental reality he almost invariably denies—"the patternlessness of life before we impose our patterns on it."

With such an aim, it was necessary to turn away from the rigidity of the fable and to employ instead a form that would allow the freedom of structure demanded by his theme. In doing so, Golding encountered a dilemma which the fabulist may avoid but one the novelist always faces. To some degree the book would have to imitate the incoherence of life and, simultaneously, approach an order or design which would make it an intelligible work of art. Though there was no means of satisfying both motives perfectly, there was at least a compromise whereby one could communicate the essential idea and still retain a kind of structure. A narrative in the first person would license the speaker to reject at the outset all of the patterns he formerly imposed on his past experience and to begin with the announced aim of discovering a new and larger understanding of his own evolution. His mission would be exploratory, unbiased by initial assumptions; and it could be allowed to end as a modest success. Thus Sammy Mountjoy, an intelligent, reputable artist who has reached middle age and a desire for reassessment of his life, broaches the task with a carefully qualified announcement of his intentions and expectations: "Not that I aspire to complete coherence. Our mistake is to clap the universe into a rationalist hat or some other. But I may find the indications of a pattern that will include me, even if the outer edges trail off into ignorance." (p. 9)

On first sight Mountjoy seems ideally suited to act as a spokesman for Golding's realism. He is not a Christian or a rationalist, a Marxist or a humanist; he has abandoned all orthodoxies as inadequate. Therefore he recognizes from the beginning what the actors in the more dramatic fables grappled with and reacted to, but never consciously grasped—the "cosmic chaos" [2] which is the basic condition of human existence. He possesses that "intransigence in the face of accepted belief" [3] which, according to Golding, the artist must have if he expects to counter the illusions of the public mind. But Mountjoy is not a professional novelist, and his motive for writing is largely personal, exploratory. The result is a surprising achievement for an amateur: there are moments of style and moments of startling insight we have no right to expect from the most thoughtful beginner; and, delighted with this interlude or that, we momentarily forgive his offenses against our staid notions of the art of narrative.

When it comes to the finished picture, however, it is not so easy to acquit him. "Time," he explains in the beginning, "is two modes. The one is an effortless perception native to us as water to the mackerel. The other is a memory, a sense of shuffle fold and coil, of that day nearer than that because more important, . . . or those three set apart, exceptional and out of the straight line altogether."

2. Golding's phrase in the interview with Owen Webster.
3. One of the requisites for the modern artist mentioned by Golding in the interview with Owen Webster.

(p. 6) Mountjoy, searching for the really vital steps in his spiritual progress, chooses the second mode. By virtue of this narrative method he gains in self-knowledge, but the reader is led through an exhausting and bewildering gymnastic routine. He is required to make leaps and to establish connections on his own power while Mountjoy, intransigent in his experiment with time, moves now forward, now backward, digging for pictures in the labyrinths of his own memories. His "story," therefore, turns out to be an illustration of the incoherence he sets out to explore. As he warned in the first chapter, this translation of incoherence into incoherence is bound to exasperate the reader. He is often forced to retreat in confusion, often forced to reread; and ultimately he is left alone to contemplate the final paradox which grows out of Mountjoy's researches: patternlessness is the only pattern. Except for this, there is nothing to cling to. There is no "fable," properly speaking, no symbolic artifice to accept or reject. *Free Fall* stands on the border between art and life. By taking up this extreme and tenuous position, it communicates, at last, the mystery and terror which transcends all fable.

Somewhere in the seemingly chartless wasteland of his past Golding's narrator made the error which is the undoing of nearly all of us: he committed himself to a specific pattern, an attitude or point of view; and in that moment of decision he lost his personal freedom. The choice, whatever it was, meant the end of innocence and a beginning of the period in his life when he incurred the burden of guilt all men seem destined to carry. In order to detect the fatal turning place, one must proceed as Mountjoy proceeds, without prejudice, and guided by no more than the faintest suspicion:

    I have hung all systems on the wall like a row of useless hats. They do not fit. They come in from outside, they are suggested patterns, some dull and some of great beauty. But I have lived enough of my life to require a pattern that fits over everything I know; and where shall I find that? Then why do I write this down? Is it a pattern I am looking for? That Marxist hat in the middle of the row, did I ever think it would last me a lifetime? What is wrong with the Christian biretta that I hardly wore at all? Nick's rationalist hat kept the rain out, seemed impregnable plate-armour, dull and decent. It looks small now and rather silly, a bowler like all bowlers, very formal, very complete, very ignorant. There is a school cap, too. I had no more hung it there . . . when I think the thing happened—the decision made freely that cost me my freedom. (pp. 6–7)

To trace the decision and its consequences is the principal motive for undertaking his personal history, but Mountjoy also hopes to communicate the tangled ambiguities of his experience. His pictures hang in the Tate Gallery. Yet these accomplishments do not satisfy him. On the limited rectangle of the canvas he has drawn perfect but isolated images which are no more than an instant of perception, "a single attitude, a selected thing," lacking the scope and sweep his understanding now craves. He remains alone in the bone globe of his skull, and he wishes to overcome his loneliness, to establish some real lines of communication between the "central darkness" he inhabits and the world outside. If one hopes both "to understand and be understood," he must create a whole series of "pictures," execute them with great caution and precision. After each is done, the "violently searching and self-condemned" artist must stand back and ask the central question: Is this the moment of loss of freedom, the moment of decision when self-consciousness and evil began? Then, taken all together, the collection may reveal how the once innocent child became the lonely and troubled man who writes.

In the first group of impressions (chapters 1–3) "no root of infection" is to be found. The bastard child who began

on Rotten Row, the boy of the pavements, is by turns
tough and loving, frightened and daring, but there is nothing in his nature or in his behavior that deserves con-
demnation. He seems to stand on some neutral ground between the extreme moral poles represented in his companions—the dreamer and childish fantasist, Johnny
Sprague; and the conniving, precocious Machiavellian,
Philip Arnold. In the eyes of the man who writes and
judges, the child is a stranger, another person entirely;
and he must be acquitted. He is found not only "innocent
of guilt" but "unconscious of innocence; happy, therefore,
and unconscious of happiness." (p. 78) There is no connection between the uncommitted boy and the self-con-
scious fallen man.

Chapters four and five are Mountjoy's *Vita Nuova,* and
here one is completely seduced by style. More than that,
there is a perfection of design which brings out every
nuance of passion and calculation in Sammy's determined
but futile attempt to possess "the glorious lady of his
mind." In reality, his Beatrice is a nineteen-year-old
schoolgirl, beautiful but dumb,[4] a kind of blessed damosel
whose "nun-like innocence" taunts and dismays her young
lover. By virtue of his promise of marriage, and even more
because he threatens to go mad with desire, she is finally
induced to give herself to him. Yet even then there can
be no real union, for the girl is rendered impotent by her
Catholic rearing and comes like a victim to the rack. Impatient, angry, and ashamed, Sammy asks her again and
again, "Don't you feel anything?" And her reply is invariably the same, "I don't know. Maybe." (p. 119) Even
so, she sacrifices herself without stint, submits to his ex-

4. Golding often links beauty and innocence. The earliest example appears in "Pish and Tush" (*Poems,* 1934) where he finds in
"lovely Lillian" a confirmation of "the rule that brainless be the
beautiful."

periments in lubricity, and allows him to make paintings of her nude body. One of them is hung publicly so that the man "can go back and see that time . . . and try to understand" what possessed him:

> There hangs the finished perfection of her sweet, cleft flesh. The light from the window strikes gold from her hair and scatters it over her breasts, her belly and her thighs. It was after the last and particularly degrading step of her exploitation; and in my self-contempt I added the electric light-shades of Guernica to catch the terror, but there was no terror to catch. There ought to have been but there was not. The electric light that ought to sear like a public prostitution seems an irrelevance. There is gold, rather, scattered from the window. There was dog faith and big eyes and submission. I look at the picture and I remember what the hidden face looked like; how after my act and my self-contempt she lay, looking out the window as though she had been blessed. (pp. 123–24)

In the rape of Beatrice's frigid and incorruptible soul the cruel lover loses his own precious innocence. The magnificent virgin becomes for him an object of curiosity, an object of lust more than love. The assault is deliberate: he chooses to impose his own will upon another being, to impose his own nature upon a creature who is patently incapable of conformity with his egotistical desire. The decision, though freely taken, makes an end of freedom and brings to his mouth the first taste of evil.

This discovery is an important one, but it concludes only the first phase of Mountjoy's effort to find and communicate the pattern that fits over his total experience. If the Beatrice episode marks the initial fall from innocence—the first symptom of a moral infection which is to rage in his blood for years to come—there remains the more difficult clinical task of tracing the causes and the consequences of that youthful fall. Is he alone to blame? Or is the world in which he grew to manhood somehow responsible as well?

At this point, *Free Fall* may be sharply distinguished from the fables, for in coming to grips with the question of environmental influence in the shaping of human mentality it embarks upon a sea of difficulties the fables could tacitly acknowledge but did not need to explore in any detail. In each of the fables Golding could afford a rather summary dismissal of the real social background and development of his characters, since the aim was to show that the perennially repeated fall of man is caused by defects inherent in his own nature. Thus the extreme situation and isolation of the castaways in *Lord of the Flies* established a pattern common to the first three books: in *The Inheritors* the sins and errors of the primitive rational man stem directly from the natural depravity of his soul or, in less orthodox terms, from the fatal limitations of his perception and intelligence; in *Pincher Martin* the ugly man on the rock is clearly the author of his own suffering. In *Free Fall,* however, Golding seems to concede that at least some of the defects of the individual are rooted in those of the society in which he comes of age. Mountjoy's narrative is exploratory rather than illustrative, novelistic rather than fabulistic; the only assumption he makes in advance is that his present consciousness is the result of a slow and subtle growth—the effect of interaction between his own nature and the social world in which that nature evolved. He is, therefore, obliged to examine the course of this dialectical process and to assign to each, the world and his own being, a just share of guilt.

Behind the premeditated exploitation of Beatrice (the first bitter fruit of his fall), there lies a decision in which his natural innocence was confounded and destroyed. But, in order to make this choice, the grasping ego of the lover first had to be confronted with alternatives. And these, surely, were not presented to his naïve and unprepared consciousness on its own authority. They were, in reality, offered to or foisted upon it by the "spiritual parents" society provides for each generation, and Mountjoy's schizophrenic world provided Nick Shales and Rowena Pringle. In Miss Pringle's classroom Sammy was exposed to the mysteries of Scripture. With the strange power accessible only to the frustrated purist, this prim virgin unraveled the fascinating adventures of the seer Moses: the man who talked with God, heard the Holy Spirit in the Burning Bush, and brought from the mountain shining absolutes— the laws of good and evil. Mr. Shales, the scientist, spoke of an entirely different universe: "A candle burnt under a bell-jar. Water rose and filled the space once occupied by oxygen. The candle went out but not before it had lighted up a universe of such orderliness and sanity that one must perforce cry: the solution to all problems is here!" (p. 212) Both systems were complete and orderly, both were beautiful. In Nick's rational universe every problem contained its own solution, and all the solutions were waiting to be discovered by the adventuresome mind of rational man. In Miss Pringle's world certainty already existed because the labor of reason had been abridged and made superfluous by the miracle of revelation. The two schoolrooms were separate, autonomous; there was no bridge between the physical and the spiritual.

In the final analysis, the schoolboy's choice had little to do with the attractions or possibilities latent in these alternatives. He was guided more by the spirit in which they were presented to him and by his own needs. Miss Pringle, agent and spokesman for the Christian universe, persecuted the boy without mercy because she was secretly in love with his homosexual warder, Father Watts Watt, and therefore jealous; but for Nick Shales, humanist, socialist, atheist, "all things were possible"—even love. He offered

that and, quite unconsciously, another irresistible induce-
ment. Sammy, like all lonely ones, wanted "the social
security of belonging to the tribe," and the tribe preferred
not only the grandiose promises of scientific humanism but
its convenient moral relativism as well. The latter, as even
the boy could see, made it possible to rationalize all of the
cruelties and animal lusts stirring in his own being: "I
saw that if man is the highest, is his own creator, then
good and evil is decided by majority vote. Conduct is not
good or bad, but discovered or got away with." (p. 218)
And so the election was made: the decision that permitted
the rape of Beatrice, the wearing of the Marxist hat, and
the gradually habitual daily acts of self-gratification which
were to make Sammy (like Pincher Martin) little more
than a mouth, or a pair of claws, bent on taking and con-
suming all that fell within his reach. He closed the door on
the world of the spirit, and Moses and Jehovah and Christ
were forgotten until the adult who mounted his own joy
above all other considerations was confined to the dark
closet in the Nazi prison camp. There, "half-crazed with
terror and despair," he made a desperate appeal to something beyond himself, an appeal for rescue; and that outcry reopened the closed door.

It is Dr. Halde, the Gestapo psychologist, who best sums
up the state of consciousness in which Captain Mountjoy
lives from day to day, but the image he draws so well is
more than Mountjoy. It is also an accurate portrait of
"modern man," the relativist, who is not even sure whether
he knows anything worth knowing:

> What embryo if it could choose, would go through the
> sufferings of birth to achieve your daily consciousness?
> There is no health in you, Mr. Mountjoy. You do not be-
> lieve in anything enough to suffer for it or be glad. There
> is no point at which something has knocked on your door
> and taken possession of you. You possess yourself. Intel-

lectual ideas, even the idea of loyalty to your country sit on you loosely. You wait in a dusty waiting-room on no particular line for no particular train. And between the poles of belief, I mean the belief in material things and the belief in a world made and supported by a supreme being, you oscillate jerkily from day to day, from hour to hour. Only the things you cannot avoid, the sear of sex or pain, avoidance of the one suffering repetition and prolongation of the other, this constitutes what your daily consciousness would not admit, but experiences as life. Oh, yes, you are capable of a certain degree of love, but nothing to mark you out from the ants or the sparrows. (pp. 144–45)

Halde's object in questioning Sammy is to learn how escapes are made from the prison compound, and he purposely selects for examination a man who is subject to temptation and capable of betrayal. He offers freedom in exchange for information; but Sammy, who cannot reveal what he does not know, is forced to endure the torture Halde has prepared as a last resort. After a few hours of solitary confinement Captain Mountjoy tortures himself into helplessness. His dark cell becomes a chamber of horrors, created *ex nihilo* by the perverse imagination of a fallen man.

This process is familiar to the reader of the fables. Left alone on the island of the self, man discovers the reality of his own dark heart, and what he discovers is too abominable for him to endure. At the highest pitch of terror he makes the only gesture he can make—a raw, instinctive appeal for help, for rescue. This time, in contrast with the negativism of *Lord of the Flies* or of *The Inheritors,* a kind of rescue comes. In the absolute darkness of what turns out to be only a harmless broom closet, the desperate prisoner loses his self-possession and pride. He becomes a mere child crying out in the darkness; and, once he is reduced to that stature, the appeal comes from his lips naturally and without reservation. It is a stark outcry to something beyond the self, beyond the world of the finite consciousness, and the moment it is uttered the door bursts open on the forgotten world of the spirit. The door actually opens. The camp commandant, opposed to Dr. Halde's treatment of a British officer, throws open the closet door and, simultaneously, releases the prisoner from the cell of his own mind.

> The commandant indicated the door back to the camp dismissively. He spoke the inscrutable words that I should puzzle over as though they were the Sphinx's riddle.
> "The Herr Doctor does not know about peoples." (p. 253)

The simple-minded commandant is right and wrong. Dr. Halde understood the nature of the human heart: he knew that Mountjoy would torture himself into submission by creating his own hell. Ironically, the psychologist's method ends in therapy. Just as Lazarus was resurrected from the grave, reborn, so Mountjoy rises from the darkness to walk again in the light of the sun. He sees with new eyes the beauty and unfathomable richness of the creation, hears a kind of heavenly music, and experiences again the glory of the vision he had lost in the moral sickness of his young manhood.

At this stage of life, however, it is too late to recapture the purity and innocence of childhood. The euphoria of the released man gives way to a new tragic awareness. Like the blind Oedipus, he is borne down by a sense of guilt for the moral crimes he committed in his pride. Thus, when the war ends, he returns to England, determined to make amends for his sins and errors. Above all, he wishes to expiate his crime against Beatrice. He discovers that she was committed to an insane asylum shortly after he rejected her. She is a hopeless case, partly a victim of heredity; and Mountjoy (though he seems to want the full blame)

is utterly helpless, forever haunted by the terrible meta-
morphosis.

Next, with the intention of bringing the truth to the
"spiritual parents" who conditioned his soul, he visits Nick
Shales and Rowena Pringle; but he finds it useless to make
the speeches he has prepared. They remain committed to
the worlds they professed long ago and neither is capable
of understanding the duality of the universe, the basic lesson their schoolboy has learned.

> All day long the trains run on rails. Eclipses are pre-
> dictable. Penicillin cures pneumonia and the atom splits to
> order. All day long, year in, year out, the daylight explana-
> tion drives back the mystery and reveals a reality usable,
> understandable and detached. The scalpel and the mirco-
> scope fail, the oscilloscope moves closer to behaviour. The
> gorgeous dance is self-contained, then; does not need the
> music which in my mad moments I have heard. Nick's uni-
> verse is real.
> All day long action is weighed in the balance and found
> not opportune nor fortunate or ill-advised, but good or evil.
> For this mode which we must call the spirit breathes through
> the universe and does not touch it; touches only the dark
> things, held prisoner, incommunicado, touches, judges, sen-
> tences and passes on.
> Her world was real, both worlds were real. There is no
> bridge. (pp. 252–53)

In these statements [5] Mountjoy sums up the result of his
search for a pattern of patterns. He fell from innocence

5. See Golding's remarks in his review of A. C. Harwood's *The
Faithful Thinker, Spectator,* CCVI (March 24, 1961), p. 410:
"there is a deep desire in the minds of people to break out of the
globe of their own skulls, and find the significance in the cosmos
that mere measurement misses. Any man who claims to have
found a bridge between the world of the physical sciences and the
world of the spirit is sure of a hearing. Is this not because most of
us have an unexpressed faith that the bridge exists, even if we
have not the wit to discover it?"

into the common schizophrenia of modern man. He oscillated from one pole to the other, from Nick's world to Pringle's world; but neither world, neither reality, has provided a resting place for his soul. His narrative experiment reveals that the ultimate reality of his experience transcends and defies the coherence of both systems. Since he has found only irrationality and incoherence, all of the hats must remain on the wall. He has discovered the terrifying patternlessness of the soul's free flight, and he must remain as he began: uncertain, unsatisfied, "a burning amateur."

The high order of awareness Mountjoy achieves places him in a unique position among Golding's characters. In *Lord of the Flies, The Inheritors,* and *Pincher Martin* we see typical human responses to the "natural chaos" of existence. As a means of rescuing himself from the patternlessness of life, man becomes mythmaker: he creates his own designs, makes his own laws, and so tries to arrest or stabilize the moving show. These projections afford a sense of control. The would-be lord of life—unable to tolerate the confusion and terror of his free fall through time—erects a cardboard bulwark to shut out the fearful mystery of the larger cosmos. For Mountjoy, however, all patterns have fallen, one after the other; he is a man without illusions, without pride. The irretrievable errors and moral crimes he committed in the Oedipal blindness of his youth cannot be forgotten, or even exorcised. The primal innocence he knew is forever lost. Yet something precious remains to him: the wonder and terror of being wholly alive in a universe which is measureless and unpredictable.

6 ‡ The illusion of innocence

In *Free Fall* Golding set out to demonstrate that the patterns we impose upon our experience cut us off from reality. This basic theme—the same theme he had pursued in one form or another since the beginning of his career—failed to get across to the majority of his critics and readers. The main reason was that most of them continued to play the role of Piggy. Looking at the experimental novel in the old one-dimensional perspective, they saw only what the prevailing convention allowed them to see. Once again, therefore, Golding was framed as an orthodox moralist who bore a striking resemblance to John Bunyan. While the most ingenious of the essays written from this point of view [1] did not explain the abrupt departure into the radical and unprecedented methods of Mountjoy's garbled narrative, the dissenters,[2] those who knew that Golding was not

1. Ian Gregor and Mark Kinkead-Weekes, "The Strange Case of Mr. Golding and His Critics," *Twentieth Century*, CLXVII (February, 1960), pp. 115–25.
2. Actually, Frank Kermode was about the only informed "dissenter." See his essay, "The Novels of William Golding," *International Literary Annual*, No. 3 (1961), pp. 26–28.

a traditional theologian, failed to push forward a convincing alternative image. As a result, *Free Fall* has remained an unpopular riddle, one which has served to encourage the critics who charge Golding with obscurity. Indeed, all of the books written since *Lord of the Flies* have seemed less and less intelligible to those who accept the established critical views. And Golding himself, on the eve of the publication of *The Spire,* appeared to be a man behind a glass wall, gesturing dimly and no longer clearly audible.

Thus it was doubly unfortunate that the new book was rumored and anticipated for more than three years before its publication in 1964. The delay allowed those who admired only *Lord of the Flies* to build up hopes that Golding would write a second thrilling story; the serious critics, unsatisfied with the last three books, looked forward to some new light on his general intentions. Judging from the initial responses, *The Spire* has not satisfied either of these expectations. It is too complex and demanding to afford excitement at the popular level, nor does it seem to be slated for immediate critical acclaim. There is a striking mastery of the highly condensed language which has mounted in beauty and precision (not to mention difficulty) ever since the first fable, but what it has to say is no more reducible to simple sum or formula than it has been in the past. These disappointments have driven most of the reviewers to work again in terms of the standing clichés about Golding's fiction,[3] and, at the most superficial narrative level, the new book seems to support this approach. It tells of Jocelin, Dean of an English cathedral, and his inspired (finally manic) dedication to the erection of a

3. See, e.g., Granville Hicks, "The Evil that Lurks in the Heart," *Saturday Review* XLVII (April 18, 1964), pp. 35–36. Probably the best review published in the United States was Frank Kermode's, "The Case for William Golding," *The New York Review of Books,* II (April 30, 1964), pp. 3–4.

crowning four-hundred-foot spire on his church. The set-
ting this time is medieval, and the protagonist is a proud
and devout Christian priest who suffers a kind of fall from
his assumed state of grace. These facts, however, suggest
very little of the central meaning. They are of no more use
than the information that Golding has lived for more than
twenty years within sight of the four-hundred-foot Gothic
spire on the great cathedral at Salisbury. The essence of
The Spire lies in the "fable," and, as before, the fable
transcends the Christian pattern which the critics would
like to impose upon it. It may be some time before Golding's new novel is understood well enough to win the recognition it really deserves.

Above all, *The Spire* deserves eminence as tragedy. Yet
this is the very recognition which is made difficult or impossible by the assumptions of the critics. In a Christian
universe genuine tragedy is ultimately precluded, for whatever befalls the erring soul of the protagonist, whatever
punishment he suffers, must sustain our faith in divine logic
and divine justice. The ambiguous man who stands between the extreme poles of good and evil may plunge
temporarily into a state resembling genuine tragic suffering; but, in the end, his suffering must be resolved or justified. The integrity of the laws of a well-ordered universe
must be preserved. The case against Golding's Dean Jocelin
is not so clear. He is neither better nor worse than his God-
given nature permits him to be: he is alternately heroic and
detestable, and he seems to live in an Euripidean universe
which is as ambiguous as his own soul. His tragedy is that
he lives to discover the folly of his Christian illusions.
When he awakens from his dream in the last days of his
life, Jocelin's pride and faith are lost. Then he experiences a climactic epiphany far more profound in scope than
the egocentric vision which led him to believe he was chosen
by God to build the spire. What he sees fills his soul with

terror and strange joy: it is a cosmos as unfathomable and mysterious as the one revealed to the heroes of Greek tragedy.

Jocelin's progress from ignorance to tragic knowledge carries him along the same line of development followed by all of Golding's protagonists. Ralph, at the end of his ordeal, grows beyond the innocent platitudes of his heritage to realize the darkness of the human heart; Lok and Fa, in the final days of their existence, eat the bitter fruit of knowledge and lose their earthly paradise; Christopher Martin, though his corrupt pride delays insight until the last possible moment, comes to see that he is the architect of his own hell. Even in *Free Fall,* which is far less schematic, Mountjoy's search for the pattern of patterns ends by illustrating the kaleidoscopic deceits of the mind as it ranges across a reality too broad and copious for the human eye. In all of these narratives, and in *The Spire* as well, the basic structure is much the same as that found in classical tragedy and described by Aristotle in the *Poetics.* The preconceived "fable" or plot traces a spiritual evolution which is "more philosophic and of graver import" than the patterns of experience available to the artist from the immediate sociological context or from historical example. Such an imaginative design affords the opportunity of reaching a more significant generalization on the nature and destiny of all men. This generalizing power is latent in the dramatic structure itself: the plot builds toward "peripety," a reversal of the initial circumstances; the protagonist suffers a "discovery" which shatters his illusions and brings him into a larger awareness than he originally possessed.

One characteristic result of this structural order is that the real depth and meaning of successive events does not emerge clearly until the protagonist makes his discovery, for only then does he enter into a state of consciousness that allows him to take a valid measure of himself and the pattern of complications in which he has been involved. Looking back from this enlightened position, he sees that what he took for reality at a given time and in a particular situation was only illusion. The clues to the truth were present, embedded in some aspect of each action and judgment he performed, but then invisible to the innocent eye. For an Athenian audience, watching a drama based on a familiar tale or legend, it was possible to enjoy this dual perspective from the very outset. Their advance knowledge of the basic fable gave rise to a rich dramatic irony. Golding's reader is not in the same advantageous position on first reading. The fable is original, and we remain blind to the multiple ironies it contains until we come into possession of the tragic knowledge which is gradually developed by the leading intelligence. We can be certain of very little until we reach the end, and then, after ignorance is overcome, we must go back to re-examine the whole pattern. During the moment-by-moment rendering of events, we share the actor's illusions, and we must wait for him to gain insight into the tragic errors he has committed.

While a great deal of the difficulty in understanding Golding's fables must be put down to this characteristic of his structures, one must still account for the almost universal complaint that, for some reason, the burden on the reader has increased since *Lord of the Flies*. A part of the answer lies in the growth of a false image of Golding and the consequent distortion of his aims, but another part of the answer has to do with the management of the point of view he broaches in *The Inheritors* and continues in the later books. Like the first novel, *The Inheritors* and *Pincher Martin* are written in the first person, but we are now forced to read without the advantage of more than one perspective on the same complex of events. Further, the omniscient interludes that formerly oriented us in the wider world appear less frequently. The effect is to carry us into what seems on first sight a narrowly subjective framework where we are obliged to concentrate with an unusual intensity on the experience and judgment of an unusual intelligence. In the course of the narrative we learn to see and think in a new way, so that when a "normal" perspective is restored in the closing chapter we are presumably ready to recognize that this shift to a "rational" view simply does not do justice to the realities encountered before. *Free Fall,* though it is written in the first person, accomplishes much the same thing. In laying out his series of pictures Mountjoy intentionally ignores chronological order, and by denying us the expected progression and order he manages to expose the realities of his spiritual evolution.

What Golding achieves, or tries to achieve, through these dramatizations of immediate perception and experience amounts to more than a shallow psychological realism. That in itself would be of little value. His narrative technique (especially in the later works) goes hand in hand with the consistent design of his fables, and it would be a futile exercise in analysis to speak of one without taking into account the other. Invariably, Golding elects as his subject a mind in crisis. Both style and structure are calculated to show how the human mind operates under extreme pressure and to show what happens when it makes some revolutionary discovery which requires abandonment of whatever assumptions and conceits dominated its experience in the past. The breakthrough, when it comes, may bring the end of a simple innocence, as in *Lord of the Flies* and *The Inheritors;* or, and this is the case in the other books, it may bring about the destruction of a long-standing adult pride. As this new reality opens before the hapless sensibility, there is not only an awakening to the limitations of one's own nature; there is also a widening sense of the tragic fate that may befall any man in an unpredictable and hopelessly ambiguous cosmos.

It is this same lesson, or revelation, that comes to the saintly Dean Jocelin at the end of *The Spire*. If most of the reviewers missed the point, it is because the scholarly critics had provided no grounds for recognition of Jocelin as a tragic hero in the Euripidean tradition. And, in the second place, the new novel is replete with all the old difficulties and obstacles to understanding. Nearly everything we see and hear is filtered through the mind of the obsessive Dean. The effect—especially in the early chapters, when he is almost wholly naïve in his Christian beliefs—is that we are given only a few vague hints of the truths lying outside the range of his perception. There are interims of dialogue where the presence of another person suggests an alternative view on things, and there are passages of objective description that etch some bold image of the larger world across the distorted impressions which form in Jocelin's mind. But, for the most part, we inhabit his being and commit his errors until his privileged hour comes. It comes only after the spire is finished and its creator lies exhausted and broken by his superhuman effort to defy nature.

The spire first appears to Jocelin in what he believes to be a holy vision, and so he begins the task of creation with the conviction that he has been chosen by God to do God's work. The secret vision is a source of unadulterated joy and a source of strength, lending to the recipient the authority and the will to override all mundane objections. From the very beginning he is met with objections, for at the practical level his model requires a construction of wood, stone, and metal rising to an improbable height over a patch of swampy ground that will not afford a secure foundation. In the original conclave of priests summoned to judge the plan, the first doubts and protests are voiced;

then the master builder digs a shallow pit, strikes mud, and declares he can proceed no further; in the village the people laugh and speak of "Jocelin's Folly." Yet the vision itself remains steadfast and unassailable because it is God-given: possessing it, and possessed by it, Jocelin drives the men of little faith against their will and better judgment. They are his "tools" as he, in turn, is the chosen tool or instrument in the hands of the Divine Master.

The first two chapters of *The Spire* cover no more than a single day in a labor that is to require two years, but the extended treatment of this brief time performs a key function in the total pattern of the narrative. It provides an illustration of the lesson or truth which the visionary, blind and perverse in his conceit, will not grasp until the very end. On this day the actual work on the spire begins, and Jocelin is swept upward on a wave of joy as the aged Lord Chancellor indicates acquiescence (really nothing more than indifference) to his plan:

> He was laughing, chin up, and shaking his head. God the Father was exploding in his face with a glory of sunlight through painted glass, a glory that moved with his movements to consume and exalt Abraham and Isaac and then God again. The tears of laughter in his eyes made additional spokes and wheels and rainbows.

> Chin up, hands holding the model spire before him, eyes half closed; joy—
> "I've waited half my life for this day!" (p. 3)

It is a moment of triumph, of pure joy, but as the hours unfold Jocelin encounters practical and moral obstacles as well as encouraging signs. Pangall, the most faithful servant of the church, complains that he is the butt of threats and vulgar jests on his impotence leveled by the rude army of workers; Roger Mason, the master builder, points out the impossibility of building so high on a foundation of mud;

and Rachel, the shrew, supports her husband's negative prognosis. She points her finger in the Dean's face, lecturing him: "there has to be as much weight under a building as there is over it. So if you are going up four hundred feet you will have to go down four hundred feet. Isn't that so, Roger?" (p. 39) Father Anselm, who voted against the spire in chapter, protests that the sanctity of the cathedral is defiled by the "dust and stink" of the workers, and Jocelin sees that he may have to pay the cost of a break with his former teacher and present confessor. But he takes an hour of prayer from the day to thank God that his "vision in stone" will be realized, and God sends an angel to comfort and aid him: "And then, quite suddenly, he knew he was not alone. It was not that he saw or heard a presence. He felt it, like the warmth of a fire at his back, powerful and gentle at the same time; and so immediate was the pressure of that personality, it might have been in his very spine." (pp. 17–18) Finally, two letters come: one is from his mother's sister, Lady Alison, a "fallen woman" who furnishes money for the spire in the hope of bribing Jocelin to grant her a tomb near the High Altar. The other is from the Lord Bishop who, visiting the Holy Father in Rome, promises to send a Holy Nail to be affixed at the pinnacle of the spire.

In the course of this first day Jocelin's soul is cast high and low. He moves through shadows into brilliant shafts of light and joy, then back into the shadows again. "He looked down at the bishop's letter. It's like a pair of scales in the market, he thought. Joy carries me up in one pan, and Anselm sinks in the other. There is the Nail and my Angel. There is the chancellor and the master builder and his wife." (p. 45) So Jocelin enters into the initial stages of the extended and tortuous dialectic which grows out of his determination to merge vision and practical labor, to impose upon recalcitrant nature the image he saw in an ecstatic dream. The dialectic is to end by exhausting all the resources of his being, but he does not foresee the appalling cost to himself and to others. In the beginning, he imagines that his will is God's will, and he builds on the foundation of this faith, this illusion. The very first hours of effort illustrate that both man and nature will oppose and eventually corrupt his pure vision. The day itself is like an open text and Jocelin like a proud and ignorant novice. As the catechism begins, he is unable to grasp the drift and import of the lesson exposed to him.

On the morning of the second day the autumn rains begin, and they do not cease in answer to Jocelin's prayers. Even the Chosen One must wait and endure with ordinary men the slow passing of the winter season. Work on the pit at the crossways of the cathedral is brought to a halt. The church itself seems like "a great stone ship" adrift on a treacherous sea, and the voices in the candle-lit chapel rise "in fear of age and death, in fear of weight and dimension, in fear of darkness and a universe without hope." (p. 50) In the passage opening the third chapter we are given one of those larger views in which we see Jocelin as he is incapable of seeing himself. In this, and in similar passages throughout the novel, the effect is to restore our sense of proper dimension: the illusions habitually projected by Jocelin's mind stand out against the background of abiding realities. The language has a unique potency because it affords a sudden flash of insight into the tragic frailty of man's self-created and protective illusions. In these lines, for example, we see Jocelin caught up in the ancient cycle of nature where his stature is reduced to the common level:

When he woke at dawn next morning, he could hear the rain, and he remembered what the master builder had said. So he prayed among other things for fine weather. But the rain came for three days, with only a half day to follow it of low cloud and soaked air; so that housewives hung what linen there was to wash before smouldering fires that dirtied more linen than they dried; and then there was wind and rain for a week. When he came out of his deanery, cloaked for a hurried passage to the cathedral, he would see the clouds at roof level so that even the battlements of the roof were blurred by them. As for the whole building itself, the bible in stone, it sank from glorification to homiletics. It was slimy with water streaming down over moss and lichen and flaking stones. When the rain drizzled, then time was a drizzle, slow and to be endured. When the rain lashed down, then the thousand gargoyles—and now men thought how their models mouldered in the graveyards of the close or the parish churches—gave vent. They uttered water as if this were yet another penalty of damnation; and what they uttered joined with what streamed down glass and lead and moulding, down members and pinnacles, down faces and squared headlands to run bubbling and clucking in the gutter at the foot of the wall. When the wind came, it did not clear the sky, but cuffed the air this way and that, a bucketful of water with every cuff, so that even a dean must stagger, pushed from behind; or leaning against a gust like a blow, find his cloak whipped out like wings. When the wind fell, the clouds fell too and he could no longer see the top half of the building; and because of the drizzle he lost the sense of the size of it. Therefore the approaching eye had to deal with a nearer thing, some corner of wet stone, huge in detail and full of imperfections, like a skin seen too close. The re-entrants on the north side—but there was no direction of light to show which was north and which south —stank with the memories of urination. The flood waters by the river, spread over the causeway, took no account of the guards at the city gate, but invaded the greasy streets. Men and women and children crouched by what fire they had and the smoke from damp logs or peat formed a haze under every roof. Only the alehouses prospered. (pp. 46–47)

From this point on, time is not reckoned with precision because Jocelin measures it only in terms of progress or delay in construction of the spire. The resistance he encounters, whether it springs from natural or from human

causes, serves largely to intensify his single-minded determination, and at times his monomania threatens to close
off the objective world entirely. There are long periods in
which we are confined to the narrow range of his consciousness. Certain events, however, break in upon his
mind and corrupt the purity of his vision. They remain as
lurid and indelible elements in the picture, forcing him to
recognize that the spiritual cost of his creation will mount
beyond his expectations.

The coming of the army of workers under Roger Mason
amounts to an invasion of the vulgar world upon the sanc-
tified island of the church. In admitting this force, Jocelin
unwittingly betrays his own kingdom. The peace and
security entrusted to his hands are immediately threatened,
and he must choose between the erection of the spire and
the well-being of his "children." He sacrifices everything
in the name of his appointed task of creation. He sees
Goody Pangall, his "daughter in God," enter the tent of
love with Roger Mason, and he sees that they are held
there in spite of their will and conscience. He listens to the
clacking Rachel, unaware of this clandestine union, explain
to him why she has no child by Roger: "it wasn't that she
was barren as some people might think and indeed had
said, my Lord, no indeed! But she *had* to laugh and then
he *had* to laugh—" (p. 54) The rising tide of natural life,
the very season of spring, strikes Jocelin as crude and
obscene; and he cries out in protest, "Filth! Filth!" But the
impurity he observes in others invades his own dreams.
The angel at his back is joined by a devil, and night after
night the devil assaults him at the loins as he dreams of
Goody and her red hair. In some recess far below the level
of his waking mind, far removed from the saintly image in
which he conceives himself, Jocelin's animal nature begins
to stir. It drives him to rationalize with all the ingenuity
at his command, to summon the comforting angel as often

as he can, and to keep before his eyes the beauty and integrity of his secret vision.

The greatest crisis comes on the day Roger Mason digs into the mud and charnel beneath the crossways to expose to view "the living, pagan earth." It is as though the "roof of hell" has been pried open, for they look down upon horrors that cannot be endured by the living. As Jocelin peers into the cellerage beneath the crust of the earth, he sees some form of hideous life that must not be exposed to the light of day. The ground is boiling with graveworms or grubs doing their silent work among the noseless men who lie buried there. He covers his mouth, makes the sign of the cross again and again; and then, spontaneously, the master builder calls out for stones to fill the pit.

Even before this discovery, Roger Mason had argued against building higher than precedent or practicality should carry him, and he now assumes that he will be released from a plan so obviously in conflict with natural law. His common sense is no match for what Jocelin calls "faith." Because there is no secure earthly foundation on which to build, he takes the whole weight of the spire on his own shoulders. In spiritual or psychological terms this means that he must sustain the burden and stress of all the anxieties and sins to be accrued in realizing his own conception. The creator's spine is the frail foundation for his own self-made world. In practical terms, it means that Roger must be asked to support the colossal spire on the four thin struts or pillars which already bear the great weight of the roof. Incredulous, he listens and protests, but Jocelin refuses to release him.

When the workers are told of the decision, a riot breaks out; and it is followed by defections from the ranks. In this melee a series of nightmare scenes are flashed before Jocelin's eyes. He sees the workers driving Pangall at the end of a broom and one of their number holding the model of the spire between his legs to mock Pangall's impotence. He sees his faithful servant break and run away, his little kingdom lost; and he sees Roger and Goody, on opposite sides of the horrible pit, acknowledge to each other the defeat of their scruples and restraint. Jocelin is both agent of and helpless witness to these acts—and to the moral damage they presage. But only by retaining the master builder can he build the spire; only by sacrificing Pangall and Goody, Roger and Rachel, can he do "his Father's business." This is what it means, he thinks, "to offer one-self and have the offer accepted." This is the awesome ex-pense of spirit one must bear when his will is "linked to a Will without limit or end."

Though every stone added to the spire increases Jocelin's burden of sin, he does not pause to calculate the stress and strain on his own being until the structure is complete. Others are not so blind. Halfway up the tower four images are to be built in to commemorate forever the spirit and visage of her creator. Gilbert, the dumb sculptor, records in these stone portraits the mounting physical and spiritual cost written on Jocelin's face. The images show "the gaunt, lifted cheekbones, the open mouth, the nostrils strained wide as if they were giving lift to the beak, like a pair of wings, the wide, blind eyes." (p. 20) The silent artist has captured the essence of Jocelin's soul: the hunter, the rapacious eagle in flight, the blind intensity of the mad-man. The visionary, rapt in his illusion, sees in this same image the grandeur and sweep of the Holy Spirit, the open mouth of an angel singing hosannas and hallelujahs. The truth held before his eyes is no more instructive to him than the daily lesson of experience which reveals the impurity, the duality, of all things in the created world. Jocelin's naïve faith in his own goodness works a meta-morphosis in everything he perceives. Innocent of his own nature, as easily deceived as a child, his mind touches all things with its own laws.

This capacity for self-deception has its roots in the past. An examination of Jocelin's personal history shows that a part of the mythmaking power of his mind may be traced simply to "human nature," and in this respect he is no different than the characters in the other fables. The great difference lies in his Christian training and beliefs. His entire life has been built on idealistic notions too pure to withstand the assault of reality, and the narrative provides a wealth of ironic contrasts and juxtapositions. All of them illustrate the uniquely Christian innocence which constitutes Jocelin's tragic flaw. The principle is always the same: in one frame we are shown his illusion; in the other, the reality. The effect is necessarily cumulative, rising to its full dramatic force only after the protagonist is brought to the point where his self-made world collapses. At the end of *The Spire,* we contemplate the tragic result of Christian naïveté.

The building of the spire, therefore, is but the climactic and crucial episode in a dream as long as Jocelin's life, and the adult is no different than the child. The figure of Anselm, for example, still retains the halo of glory which the romantic youth projected onto the master of novices. He remembers "the cloister by the sea, the flashing water, the sun and sand," and his heart is troubled by a mixture of love and grief when Anselm opposes the spire. In the final hour of revelation the image fades as Jocelin learns the truth: that Anselm was only irritated by his "adolescent regard"; that Anselm burned with jealousy as his former pupil rose through the ranks; that Anselm, through calculation and connivance, will succeed him as Dean.

Of greater consequence is the tragic injustice which grows out of Jocelin's puristic conception of Goody, his "daughter in God." After she blossoms into young womanhood he still prefers to think of her as the angelic child, and he prefers to think of himself as a spiritual father and protector of her virginal sweetness and innocence. Only in the final hour of revelation does he see the realities behind this romantic façade: that he loved her with all his being; that he arranged her marriage to the impotent Pangall as a means of preserving her virginity for himself; that he denied her fulfillment of her own nature; that his "daughter in God" has been mistress of his flesh and, through the medium of his unholy pride, transformed into the red-haired "witch" of his own phallic dreams.

The same dreams, though he held them secret, expressed themselves in the ecstasy of his waking vision. The saint kneeling in the chapel was at the same time the sinner and the fool of his own dark heart. The model of the spire itself suggests the dimension of his nature that he has always denied: "The model was like a man lying on his back. The nave was his legs placed together, the transepts on either side were his arms outspread. The choir was his body; and the Lady Chapel, where now the services would be held, was his head. And now also, springing, projecting, bursting, erupting from the heart of the building, there was its crown and majesty, the new spire." (p. 4) While the spire is in part the phallus of Jocelin's dreams, it does not follow that his entire effort of creation amounts to no more than a covert expression of his sexual nature.[4] It does mean, however, that *The Spire* repeats one of Golding's fundamental themes. Jocelin's discovery of the "cellarage" beneath the surface of his own mind [5] constitutes the first injury to his

4. One anonymous reviewer writes that "Golding insistently suggests that it may just as well be a phallic sublimation of Jocelin's repressed yearning for the red-haired wife of a cathedral worker," but this is too simplistic to summarize Golding's intentions. See *Time,* LXXXIII (April 24, 1964), pp. 104–06.

5. The cellar metaphor first appears in *Pincher Martin* (p. 138), where it is used to suggest the morbidity and horror lurking be-

pride: it forces him to contemplate the relationship between the spirit and the flesh, between the head and the
heart, and to accept the fact that no man can justly claim
to be innocent of his own nature. Still, this discovery of his
own fallibility is only one aspect of the tragic knowledge he
gains in the hour of his death.

When the Visitor arrives from Rome with the Holy Nail
he finds a disheveled and half-mad priest who does the
work of the Devil in the name of God. A kind of trial en-
sues, and Jocelin is charged with crimes against his sacred
office. Largely on the evidence given by Anselm, his confessor, he is deprived of his responsibilities as Dean of the
cathedral. To all of this he remains indifferent, until he
performs his last act of faith. It consists of driving the
Nail into the very point of the finished spire, as if the useless relic could hold the leaning structure against the sky.
Then, when he comes down, the work is finished and he
begins to awaken from his manic dream.

He lies helplessly in bed, exhausted and sick, and here
"the new knowledge" begins to seep into his mind. He
rises only two more times, each occasion bringing him a
step closer to death and revelation. On the first occasion,
he rises to see Lady Alison (whose urgent letters he has
ignored) and to hear her plea for an honorable grave in his
church. Adamant against her—though, in reality, her sins

---

neath the conscious self. In *The Spire* the same metaphor is used
with greater elaboration and better effect. Jocelin, after his fall
from pride, is described as "a building about to fall"; and, in his
useless confession to Roger Mason, he asks: "What's a man's mind,
Roger? Is it the whole building, cellarage and all?" (p. 205) This
need not be taken to mean the "original evil" lurking in the dark
heart of man. It signifies, rather, that human pride wishes to deny
any connection with the death, decay, and corruption apparent
in all nature. We like to think of the "spirit" as separate, immacu-
late, and immortal; but in Golding's world spirit and flesh, spirit
and nature, are one indivisible entity.

do not equal his own—he replies, "There's a sense in which your body would—forgive me—defile it." As her anger rises he tries to explain the thing he imagines so hard for a "fallen woman" to understand: that he was chosen, chosen by God, and that his work has made the ground sacrosanct. He is shocked by a peal of laughter, more shocked by the story she has to tell: "Listen, nephew, *I* chose you." And choose him she did. As mistress to the King in her youth, she was offered a gift; and she elected to favor Jocelin as a means of triumphing over her pious and disapproving sister. The King said: " 'We shall drop a plum in his mouth.' Just like that. Casually. And then I said: 'He's a novice, I believe, in some monastery or other.' I started to giggle, and he started to roar with laughter and then we were hugging each other and rolling over and over—because you must admit it was not without its funny side. We were both young, after all. It appealed to us. Jocelin—?" (pp. 177–78)

His pride broken by the knowledge that his "divine" appointment was conceived on the King's couch, Jocelin rises from his bed to seek forgiveness from Roger Mason. He finds him sick and drunk, a useless man with a reputation as a dangerous builder, and so filled with hatred and anguish that he can neither receive nor grant true forgiveness. Jocelin leaves the builder's house only to be stoned in the streets of the village (his punishment is thorough), and then he finds himself facing the ceiling of his room again. Lying on his twisted back, staring upward like one already dead, he reviews his crimes. He thinks of Pangall's flight, of Goody's death in childbirth, of Roger's bitterness, and of Rachel's humiliation. Summing up, performing judgment on himself, he thinks: "I traded four people for a stone hammer." He says almost nothing to those who bend over him. Communication is broken now, because he finds speech too complex, because he has access to only one mouth; and one mouth is not enough to articulate what he has learned of his own nature, the nature of others, and the nature of God's world.

These three aspects of his enlarged knowledge compose but a single vision in the last moments of his life, a vision so great in magnitude that it cannot pass through the narrow channel of mind and lips. Jocelin struggles to leave behind, for the others, some fragment of the truth he sees, but the words that form in his mind are too small to encompass it. We know that he sees his own ridiculous frailty and that of all men. They appear to him as extraordinary, parchment-covered creatures, hollow men held erect by "a mad structure of bones"; and, perceiving this, he thinks: *"How proud their hope of hell is. There is no innocent work. God knows where God may be."* (p. 214) But the rest is too large for his mind, and we are held in his mind until the light of consciousness goes out.

The vision is captured, therefore, only in vague symbolic images, in metaphors which the fading soul of a disillusioned Christian would naturally select. A few days before his death he saw in the garden close a blooming apple tree and a blue kingfisher flying like an arrow through the flawless sky. He thinks of his soul now as a bird flying through "the panic-shot darkness," and he struggles vainly to say the "words of magic and incomprehension": *"It's like the apple tree!"* He envisions the creation and the life he has lived in the image of the apple tree blooming in the garden, but now he knows that "there was more to the apple tree than one branch." It held the fruit of good and evil, and he partook of both as the first man did, as all men do. The words are not enough; they do not even reach the air. But they have to do. No man could find the words to tell us what it is to see God. At this juncture, Father

Adam leans over, and he sees the tremor of the lips which he interprets as a cry of "God! God! God!" Then, out of the charity and pride to which he has access as one of the living, he lays the useless Host on the dead man's tongue.

7 ‡ *The greater reality*

Through tragic suffering Dean Jocelin is brought to the very pinnacle of spiritual development, and in the last moments of his life he experiences a vision befitting the death of a true saint. Appropriately enough, the language rises in poetic intensity as it tries to capture something of the greater reality which lies beyond the familiar levels of comprehension. But, during these privileged moments of revelation, Jocelin's mind seems to flicker helplessly between joy and terror. We know that he looks out upon a prospect too magnanimous to be fathomed or endured by the finite consciousness, a universe so broad and ambiguous that even the radical and highly condensed images which occur to the ecstatic priest can offer no more than a vague impression. We hear only a few notes of heavenly music, as it were. They are intriguing but flawed and incomplete, and then all fades into silence.

This language, of course, is not really new. We have heard it before, in the other novels, and on similar occasions. Much of the genius of Golding's fiction lies in the power of his language to render the immediate experience of the perceiving mind as it moves through the various phases of its struggle to impose one pattern or another on a cosmos that cannot be reduced to human proportions. He often utilizes what might be called a language of psychological crisis, and, in keeping with the structure of his novels, it reaches the highest pitch of intensity as it attempts to communicate some climactic insight on the part of the protagonist.

Ingenious as it may be, Golding's effort to dramatize the immediate psychological life of his characters has created some formidable difficulties for his readers and critics. The later novels (in which he has tended to minimize the role of omniscient narrator) have put an unusual burden on his interpreters. The response has not been favorable: Golding's popularity has declined, and some of the more serious critics have raised the charge of obscurity. What is the rationale behind his use of language, especially in the later novels? To what extent, and on what grounds, are his critics justified in leveling the charge of obscurity? The answers to these questions may establish a more secure basis than we now have for a really fair assessment of Golding's accomplishment; and, finally, the answers may also suggest some vital perspectives which the critics have hardly begun to explore.

At least a part of the rationale behind Golding's meticulous concern with the language of his novels can be deduced from his scattered remarks on the general nature of contemporary fiction. Some of these are found in essays which, on first sight, seem only thinly related to the art of fiction. "On the Crest of the Wave," [1] for example, launches an attack on universal education and, in particular, our blind faith in the efficacy of scientific method and the value of technological skill on which it is based. We have hopelessly

---

1. *Times Literary Supplement* (June 17, 1960), p. 387.

confused the great power given to us by scientific method with the power to make value judgments, and the latter, according to Golding, should be the chief aim of education. One readily observable effect of the new education is a sharp decline in the ability to use and to understand language. The artist who expects to keep in touch with such a mentality is obliged to lower his standards of communication, and this is precisely what has been done by a great number of modern novelists. They have abandoned the richly textured language formerly expected of the literary artist to take up instead the bleak and limited idiom which insures communication with their audience. Nor is it simply a matter of language. These novelists have adopted the underlying assumptions of scientific and pseudoscientific method. We see them utilizing the techniques of the sociologist or the psychologist, and doing so, apparently, with the belief that these emerging disciplines afford a better means to accurate description or analysis of human motives and behavior than the writer has available to him in literary tradition.

In a statement of his own creed as a novelist [2] Golding sketches in a little more of the philosophical basis for his own practice, and he also points to the reasons for his sense of alienation from the mode of fiction which has prospered in our technological society. The "true business" of the novelist, he argues, is not description of behavior or "current affairs." Contemporary life is only the visible expression of "the basic human condition" which the novelist ignores at enormous cost to the integrity and durability of his art. If we observe in his work "a serious, an Aeschylean, preoccupation with the human tragedy, that is only to say that he is committed to looking for the root of the disease instead of the symptoms." And the source of the "disease"

2. *London Magazine,* IV (May, 1957), pp. 45–46.

is not to be found in what science has taught us to call the "objective world," but rather in the nature of the observer himself. Modern man, endowed with conceits that render him blind to his own limitations, suffers from an "appalling ignorance of his own nature." Thus the most vital function of the novelist today is to dramatize the life of the mythmaking mind, to show it struggling in some crisis which threatens both its primal innocence and acquired ignorance, and, in the climactic moment, to bring it into recognition of its own folly.

In order to fulfill his task Golding writes novels so highly stylized and so rigidly structured that they take on the characteristics we associate with poetry,[3] and this fact sets his work apart from much of the fiction produced today. It is also the main source of confusion and frustration on the part of most of his critics. Unaccustomed to the demands made upon them by Golding's difficult prose, they have charged him with obscurity; baffled by the absence of the expected sociological chronicle, they have accused him of turning his back on the modern world. Neither of these charges is likely to withstand the test of time. At least half of the obscurities complained of have been fabricated by the critics themselves, and the notion that Golding is out of touch with his own world is little more than a reflection of the glib and impatient response to his techniques.

A few have seen the picture in another light. Steven Marcus,[4] in a speculative essay on recent trends in the novel, maintains that Golding is more precocious than out of date. His novels are written "according to what we can describe as a poetic conception both of experience and of

3. In a speech before the National Council of Teachers of English (San Francisco, November, 1963) Golding stressed the basic kinship between the language of the poet and the language of the novelist.

4. "The Novel Again," *Partisan Review*, XXIX (Spring, 1962), pp. 179–84.

the shape which experience must take," and this same conception, Marcus suggests, is behind the "rigorously organ-
ized and heavily controlled" short novels of certain other
contemporaries. In the fiction of Bernard Malamud, for example, one observes a similar condensation. There is enough
evidence to suggest that these writers may represent the
beginning of a revolution in novelistic form.

The tendency Marcus observes in recent fiction in English is already an accomplished fact among the writers of
the *nouvelle vague* in France. It is not merely refreshing,
but potentially very useful, to think of Golding in relation
to their work, as avant-garde, instead of seeing him always
in the image of the old-fashioned moralist who wants to
tell us about the fox and the crow once again. There is no
evidence that he has read the novels (or anti-novels) of the
French experimentalists, but he certainly evidences the
same preoccupation with mind as maker of its own world.
For Golding, the human eye is like the shutter of a camera:
it opens on this perspective and on that perspective, admitting to the "central darkness" within a confusing multi-
plicity of "pictures" which the fumbling and limited intelligence tries to arrange in meaningful patterns. Robbe-Gril-
let, in an analogous metaphor, personifies the human mind
as a voyeur spying into the ostensibly objective world but
(neurotically) unable to distinguish between what it sees and
what it wishes to see, between fact and fantasy. Both novelists are bent on examining the various planes of reality projected or perceived by the mind as it plunges through experience and time in a state of free fall.

Golding, however, probably owes nothing to his literary
contemporaries in France. He has warned us that he stands
more or less isolated from the literature of his time. On the
one hand, his ideas and techniques look back to the tradition of Greek tragedy (and there is some special allegiance
to Euripidean psychology); on the other hand, he is also in

touch with modern science.[5] It is from this quarter that he seems to derive the semicubistic or geometrical technique we observe most readily in *Free Fall*. The same novel evidences a concern with our inability to generalize effectively or to discover stable "laws" in a universe which is constantly expanding and assuming different shapes according to the theoretical post of observation we choose to occupy. The problem of relativity, which Golding knows about through his reading in contemporary science, is here illustrated on the psychological level. In fact, all of the carefully structured narratives are taken up with the progress of the leading intelligence toward a tragic knowledge of its own limitations, and, like *The Spire,* they all end in a disillusionment that opens a first view into a cosmos which is simply too large for human measurement or control.

But we are never given more than a glimpse into this cosmos. When the great moment comes, the language surges upward to capture the hysteria, the sense of dangerously widening borders, as the formerly naïve mentality of the protagonist suffers a prodigious growth. Then, with the end of "innocence" and the collapse of all the false patterns and conceits, the psychological drama comes to an end. Mountjoy alone begins in mature disillusionment, but he is burdened with guilt and intent upon analysis of the sins of the past. We learn only a little (all too little) about the psychological or philosophical present from which he

5. In a recent letter to me Golding remarked: "though a few years ago it was true I'd read little but Greek for twenty years, it's true no longer. The Greek is still there and I go back to it when I feel like that; now I must get in some sort of touch with the contemporary scene, and not necessarily the literary one; the scientific one perhaps." One can always hope that Golding will also get acquainted with literary existentialism. It might suggest to him that tragic disillusionment is more common than he seems to think and that some of the complaint about his fables comes from those who want him to begin his story where he customarily ends—i.e., with a realization of our existential condition.

speaks. He tells us in his prefatory apology for the narrative that he is "a burning amateur," "torn" and terrified by the patternlessness, the incoherence, of both past and present; but this is hardly satisfying. He goes on to recount his fall from childish innocence, and we get nothing more.

It is a familiar story that Mountjoy tells. It is much the same story that Golding has written several times and in several ways, yet this repetition and admirable versatility have led to an impasse in understanding. Into what kind of world do we awake if we survive spiritual adolescence and live on to look about us with a disillusioned eye? This is the fateful question which emerges from Golding's fiction, and no amount of critical effort and speculation is going to provide a satisfactory answer. Golding himself must finally admit us into the reality beyond innocence and ignorance. For the old vein is now more or less exhausted. We have been shown the end of innocence many times; we have been shown our capacity for mythmaking. Now it is legitimate to ask what lies beyond the bitter epiphanies which bring an end to the fabled youth of the soul. Until that story is told, those who are not among the innocent must stand and wait or turn away in impatience.

So far, however, Golding has dedicated his art to exposure of the accepted beliefs or myths which possess the public mind. Those who are no longer bound by these gilded visions, those who are truly contemporary, will find no satisfaction in still another fable of innocence. They may recognize Golding for his accomplishment as a stylist; they may acknowledge him as a profound psychologist; but they may also conclude that he has little to say to them at the philosophical level. Ralph, after all, survives the island nightmare and the illusions of his heritage. What will he do after his tears subside and he faces up to the real world? Surely he is not obliged to repeat all the old errors. If this were so, he would be a helpless being in a universe rigidly structured to insure his defeat; and, in such a grimly deterministic world, what Golding has called "tragic knowledge" would be worthless. That would be darkly nihilistic, indeed. There is another alternative. Even the disillusioned mind knows that new visions spring, however absurdly, from the better part of our nature.

Bibliography

Publications by William Golding are chronologically listed below. The list is not quite complete. He recalls a short story entitled "The Anglo-Saxon" and "a few stray poems," but it was not possible to trace these items. The list of secondary studies is by no means complete. It does contain many sources useful to the scholar.

I. WILLIAM GOLDING

Poems, London: Macmillan's Contemporary Poets, 1934.

Lord of the Flies, London: Faber and Faber Ltd., 1954.

The Inheritors, London: Faber and Faber Ltd., 1955.

Pincher Martin, London: Faber and Faber Ltd., 1956.

"Envoy Extraordinary," in *Sometime, Never: Three Tales of Imagination* by William Golding, John Wyndham, and Mervyn Peake (New York: Ballantine Books, 1956), pp. 3–60. Published simultaneously by Eyre Books, London.

London Magazine, IV (May, 1957), pp. 45–46. A brief statement of creed in a series by modern writers called "The Writer in His Age."

"Pincher Martin," *Radio Times*, CXXXVIII (March 21, 1958), p. 8. Golding's own brief explanation of *Pincher Martin*.

The Brass Butterfly, London: Faber and Faber Ltd., 1958.

Free Fall, London: Faber and Faber Ltd., 1959.

"The Ladder and the Tree," *The Listener*, LXIII (March 24, 1960), pp. 531–33.

"On the Crest of the Wave," *Times Literary Supplement* (June 17, 1960), p. 387.

"Miss Pulkinhorn," *Encounter,* XV (August, 1960), pp. 27–32.

"In Retreat," *Spectator,* CCIV (March 25, 1960), pp. 448–49. Review of Raleigh Trevelyan's *A Hermit Disclosed.*

"Raider," *Spectator,* CCIV (May 20, 1960), p. 741. Review of Samuel Eliot Morison's *John Paul Jones.*

"Islands," *Spectator,* CCIV (June 10, 1960), pp. 844–46. Review of *The Swiss Family Robinson* and *Treasure Island.*

"Headmasters," *Spectator,* CCV (August 12, 1960), p. 252. Review of T. W. Bamford's *Thomas Arnold.*

"In My Ark," *Spectator,* CCV (September 16, 1960), p. 409. Review of Gavin Maxwell's *The Ring of Bright Water.*

"Man of God," *Spectator,* CCV (October 7, 1960), p. 530. Review of Lesley Blanch's *The Sabres of Paradise.*

"Prospect of Eton," *Spectator,* CCV (November 25, 1960), pp. 856–57. Review of Christopher Hollis's *Eton.*

"Billy the Kid," *Spectator,* CCVI (November 25, 1960), pp. 808 ff. A personal essay which recalls early school days.

"Thin Partitions," *Spectator,* CCVI (January 13, 1961), p. 49. Review of Russell Brain's *Some Reflections on Genius and Other Essays.*

"Rise of Love," *Spectator,* CCVI (February 10, 1961), p. 194. Review of John Bayley's *The Characters of Love.*

"Androids All," *Spectator,* CCVI (February 24, 1961), pp. 263–64. Review of Kingsley Amis's *New Maps of Hell.*

"All or Nothing," *Spectator,* CCVI (March 24, 1961), p. 410. Review of *The Faithful Thinker,* a collection of essays on Rudolf Steiner, ed. by A. C. Harwood.

"Before the Beginning," *Spectator,* CCVI (May 26, 1961), p. 768. Review of Grahame Clark's *World Prehistory.*

"Astronaut by Gaslight," *Spectator,* CCVI (June 9, 1961), pp. 841–42. Review of eight tales by Jules Verne.

"It's a Long Way to Oxyrhynchus," *Spectator,* CCVII (July 7, 1961), p. 9. A personal essay which recalls Golding's early attempts to imitate the style of other writers.

"Party of One: Thinking as a Hobby," *Holiday,* XXX (August, 1961), pp. 8 ff.

"Tolstoy's Mountain," *Spectator,* CCVII (September 8, 1961), pp. 325–26. Review of *War and Peace.*

"Touch of Insomnia," *Spectator,* CCVII (October 27, 1961), pp. 569–70. First in a series of four articles on Golding's year as writer-in-residence at Hollins College, Virginia.

"Glass Door," *Spectator,* CCVII (November 24, 1961), pp. 732–33. Second in the series on the year's stay at Hollins College.

"English Channel," *Holiday,* XXX (November, 1961), pp. 32 ff.

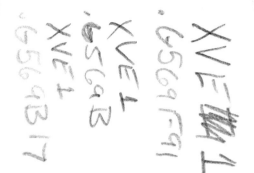

XVE ~~1~~

.6569F9J

XVE1

65CQB

XVE1

.65698.

65CQB17

"Body and Soul," *Spectator,* CCVIII (January 19, 1962), pp. 65–66. Third in the series on the year's stay at Hollins College.

"Through the Dutch Waterways," *Holiday,* XXXI (January, 1962), pp. 58 ff.

"Shakespeare's Birthplace," *Holiday,* XXXI (May, 1962), pp. 82 ff.

"Gradus ad Parnassum," *Spectator,* CCIX (September 7, 1962), pp. 327–29. Fourth and last in the series on the year's stay at Hollins College.

"Surge and Thunder," *Spectator,* CCIX (September 14, 1962), p. 370. Review of Homer's *Odyssey,* trans. by Robert Fitzgerald.

Break My Heart, a drama presented as a British Broadcasting Corporation Radio Feature Program, 1962. Remains unpublished.

"Digging for Pictures," *Holiday,* XXXIII (March, 1963), pp. 86 ff.

The Spire, London: Faber and Faber Ltd., 1964.

II. SECONDARY STUDIES

Amis, Kingsley, *New Maps of Hell,* New York: Ballantine Books, 1960.

A thorough study of science fiction which ranks Golding as an unusually serious and intelligent writer in this school.

Baker, James R. and Arthur P. Ziegler, Jr. (eds.), *Casebook Edition of William Golding's "Lord of the Flies": Text, Criticism, and Notes,* New York: G. P. Putnam's Sons, 1964.

Contains the major essays on *Lord of the Flies,* original contributions by J. T. C. Golding and others, scholarly notes by the editors, and a checklist of sixty items relevant to the novel.

Books and Art (March, 1958), n.p.

An interview in which Golding describes his aim in *Free Fall.*

Drew, Philip, "Second Reading," *Cambridge Review,* LXXVIII (1956), pp. 78–84.

A sound, if somewhat elementary, analysis of symbolism in *Lord of the Flies.*

Epstein, E. L., "Notes on *Lord of the Flies,*" in *Lord of the Flies,* New York: Capricorn Books, 1959, pp. 249–55.

Some biographical notes on Golding and a dubious "Freudian" interpretation of the novel. Contains Golding's own statement on the theme and moral intended.

Forster, E. M., "Introduction," in *Lord of the Flies,* New York: Coward-McCann, Inc., 1962, pp. ix–xii.

A brief but perceptive commentary by a man who understands Golding's allegorical method.

Freedman, Ralph, "The New Realism: The Fancy of William Golding," *Perspective,* X (Summer–Autumn, 1958), pp. 118–28.

> A somewhat obscure commentary on the first four novels, but the only essay which clearly recognizes Golding's philosophical realism.

Gindin, James, " 'Gimmick' and Metaphor in the Novels of William Golding," *Modern Fiction Studies,* VI (Summer, 1960), pp. 145–52. Reprinted in Gindin's *Postwar British Fiction,* Berkeley: University of California Press, 1962, pp. 196–206.

> An interesting but somewhat abortive attempt to understand the function of the final chapters in the first four novels. Fails to see that final chapters are written from the rationalist's point of view and that they *intentionally* contradict the "fable" as means of achieving irony.

Green, Peter, "The World of William Golding," *A Review of English Studies,* I (April, 1960), pp. 62–72.

> A general survey praising the first four novels as the best in England during the postwar years. Discusses some possible sources for *The Inheritors, Pincher Martin,* and *The Brass Butterfly.*

Gregor, Ian and Mark Kinkead-Weekes, "The Strange Case of Mr. Golding and His Critics," *Twentieth Century,* CLXVII (February, 1960), pp. 115–25.

> The best analysis of *Free Fall,* even though Golding emerges as a Christian theologian.

————, "Introduction," in *Lord of the Flies.* London: Faber and Faber School Editions, 1962, pp. i–xii.

> One of the best introductions to the novel. The editors' "Notes" (pp. 249–63) contain definitions of the schoolboy slang obscure to most American readers.

Hynes, Samuel, *William Golding,* New York & London: Columbia University Press, 1964.

> Some forty pages of generally accurate commentary in the Columbia Essays on Modern Writers series under the editorship of William York Tindall. Hynes sees that Golding is not a moralist or Christian fabulist but author of novels which belong, "not with Aesop's fables, but with the important symbolic novels of our century—with Camus's and Kafka's."

Karl, Frederick R., "The Novel as Moral Allegory: The Fiction of William Golding, Iris Murdoch, Rex Warner, and P. H. Newby," in *The Contemporary English Novel,* New York: The Noonday Press, 1962.

> A negative appraisal arguing that Golding is an amateur existentialist and a somewhat boring allegorist who would be

more appealing if he gave up the heavy-handed moralizing of his fables.

Kearns, Francis E., "Salinger and Golding: Conflict on the Campus," *America*, CVIII (January 26, 1963), pp. 136–39.

A negative estimate ranking Golding as a pessimist and a "conservative" opposed to the liberal-humanistic tradition represented by Salinger.

Kermode, Frank, "The Novels of William Golding," *International Literary Annual*, No. 3 (1961), pp. 11–29.

The best general survey of the first four novels. Reprinted in Kermode's *Puzzles and Epiphanies*, New York: Chilmark Press, 1962.

———, "The Case for William Golding," *The New York Review of Books*, XI (April 30, 1964), pp. 3–4.

The most perceptive review of *The Spire*.

——— and William Golding, "The Meaning of it All," *Books and Bookmen*, V (October, 1959), pp. 9–10. Unedited copy of the BBC radio interview of September, 1959.

Before the publication of *Free Fall*, but still one of the most valuable keys to the first three novels. The auspicious title was not authorized by Golding or Kermode.

"Lord of the Campus," *Time*, LXXIX (June 22, 1962), p. 64.

Golding comments on *Lord of the Flies*, American students, "original evil," and declares he has read "absolutely no Freud."

Marcus, Steven, "The Novel Again," *Partisan Review*, XXIX (Spring, 1962), pp. 171–95.

Argues that Golding's novels evidence the general tendency of contemporary fiction: poetic compression in both style and structure.

Nelson, William (ed.), *William Golding's "Lord of the Flies": A Source Book*. New York: The Odyssey Press, Inc., 1963.

Contains some of the early (and quite insipid) reviews, a few of the major essays, and a section of "Related Readings," offering excerpts from *Coral Island*, Hobbes, Rousseau, Frazer, Freud, Jung, etc.

Niemeyer, Carl, "The Coral Island Revisited," *College English*, XXII (January, 1961), pp. 241–45.

Analysis of Golding's use of Ballantyne's *Coral Island* in *Lord of the Flies*.

Peter, John, "The Fables of William Golding," *Kenyon Review*, XIX (Autumn, 1957), pp. 577–92.

The first serious essay on Golding published in America. Establishes the distinctions between "fiction" and "fable" which influenced most subsequent criticism.

Rosenfield, Claire, "Men of a Smaller Growth: A Psychological Analysis of William Golding's *Lord of the Flies*," *Literature and Psychology*, XI (Autumn, 1961), pp. 83–101.

> Approaches the novel through Freudian theory and jargon but arrives at useful insights into character and the ritual hunts. A revised and superior version appears in the *Casebook Edition of William Golding's "Lord of the Flies,"* ed. by James R. Baker and Arthur P. Ziegler, Jr.

"The Art of Darkness," *Time*, LXXXIII (April 24, 1964), pp. 104–06.

> A perceptive review of *The Spire* which points out the phallic symbolism involved in Dean Jocelin's vision.

Wain, John, "Lord of the Agonies," *Aspect*, I (April, 1963), pp. 56–57.

> Surveys the first four novels as Christian allegory and chides Golding for unnecessary obscurity and narrative "tricks" on the reader.

Young, Wayland, "Letter from London," *Kenyon Review*, XIX (Summer, 1957), pp. 477–82.

> Argues that first three novels are praiseworthy, except for "trick ending" device of final chapters, most offensive in *Pincher Martin*.

Index